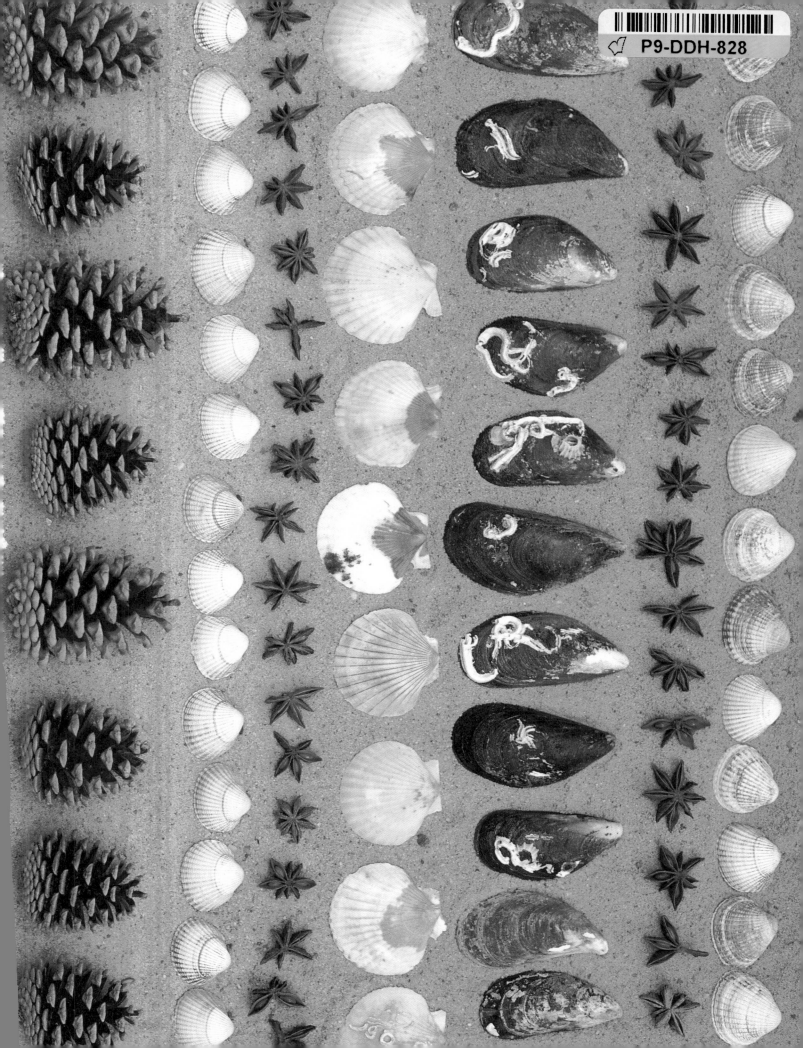

NATURAL DECORATING

natural
DECORATING

Sophisticated simplicity with natural materials

Elizabeth Wilhide and Joanna Copestick

Special photography by James Merrell, produced by Susan Skeen

CONRAN OCTOPUS

First published in 1995 by
Conran Octopus Limited
37 Shelton Street
London WC2H 9HN

Art Editor: Leslie Harrington
Illustrator: Carolyn Jenkins
Special Photography: James Merrell
(photographer), Susan Skeen (producer)
Project Editor: Denny Hemming
Copy Editor: Wendy Dallas
Assistant Editor: Jane Chapman
Picture Researcher: Rachel Davies
Production Controller: Julia Golding
Indexer: Vicki Robinson
Endpapers: Steve Wright
(Tel: 0181-299 3164)

British Library Cataloguing-in-
Publication Data
A catalogue record of this book is available
from the British Library

ISBN 1 85029 716 9

Printed and bound in China

CONTENTS

THE NATURAL LOOK

THE LURE OF NATURE HAS NEVER BEEN STRONGER. *Authentic, robust, practical and revitalizing, natural decorating is not so much a style, more a way of life. Today, trends in decorating come and go at a confusing rate; a style that might once have defined a decade is now outmoded in a season. To have been a dedicated follower of interior fashion over the past ten years would have required considerable reserves of time and money, not to mention an unflagging appetite for change. This accelerated pace cannot help but encourage a superficial attitude to the interior, as one look after another is flung off in favour of the latest fad.*

Natural decorating, by contrast, takes a long view. Materials that age well and improve with the years, furnishings that bring comfort, simplicity and practicality to the forefront, timeless surfaces and finishes that are both easy on the eye and environmentally friendly provide an antidote to the pressures of life. There will always be room for novelty, but we are beginning to appreciate the value of rooms that serve as real backgrounds for living rather than as stage sets for conspicuous consumption.

The strength of this approach lies in its versatility. Like clothing that allows the personality of the individual wearer to shine through, natural decorating works in many different contexts, enhancing basic qualities of light and space rather than imposing a grand fashion statement. In country settings, where homespun materials reinforce the link between indoors and out, the natural look makes perfect sense. Elegantly understated in traditional period rooms, fresh and positive in more contemporary surroundings, natural decorating transcends conventional distinctions between town and country, period and modern, exotic and vernacular.

The matt, chalky colours of natural paints and rich earth or vegetable tones of natural dyes, the easy-going sympathy of wood, stone and terracotta, the refined simplicity of linen, calico, muslin, wicker and raffia are all elements

Natural cane matting is suspended on a metal frame to provide an informal awning (ABOVE).

Painted handwoven baskets have a textured warmth and make a beautiful disguise for everyday clutter (LEFT).

Bamboo is a strong, quick-growing, easily sustainable cane which is widely used as a building material in the Far East. Its mellow ochre colouring and gently mottled texture bring a calm and colourful order to this simple beach house. Exposed wooden beams and bamboo poles interspersed with timber boarding provide geometric patterns which are decorative in their own right.

that have a long history of use in interior decoration. Today, the traditional virtues of such natural ingredients are ripe for rediscovery. As ecological awareness sharpens, natural decorating provides the added satisfaction of creating a healthier environment and making better use of resources.

Reasons to be natural

In recent years, interest in historical forms of decorating has grown and grown, bringing a greater awareness of the variety, refinement and artistry of old skills and methods. For those who have grown up with the notion that painting simply consists of pouring emulsion (latex) into a tray and rolling it onto the wall, the subtlety of these all but forgotten techniques has been a revelation. Equally surprising is the discovery that it is not merely the methods that are responsible for such evocative effects, but also the basic ingredients, and that despite its many disadvantages, a distempered wall, for example, has infinitely more character than one coated with vinyl silk emulsion.

It is a mistake, as historians of interior decoration would point out, to confuse historically authentic methods and materials with 'natural' ones. This is particularly true of paint. There is nothing natural, in the sense of harmless or healthy, about lime, arsenic, lead or mercury, all common components of early finishes and pigments. Our ancestors simply did not have access to or knowledge of the industrial processes that supply us with the huge range of synthetic materials to be found in every corner of our homes today, from the fibres in our carpets to the polish on our furniture. In the past, people built, decorated and furnished their homes with what was to hand, which of necessity was what the earth produced: animal, vegetable or mineral. Materials harvested, mined, hewn or quarried locally were used to create buildings that effectively grew out of the landscapes in which they were sited.

Modern synthetic products have delivered enormous short-term advantages. They are often, though not always, cheaper and they have generally been designed to offer a number of specific practical benefits: easy care, easy application or installation, and resistance to abrasion, infestation or rot.

The disadvantages of these materials, however, take a little time to understand. You only have to spend a day wearing a nylon shirt to appreciate the superiority of cotton, but the drawbacks of nylon fibres in your carpeting may take longer to discover. When choosing clothing, we are drawn to natural materials, which feel better on the skin and which soften and wear attractively. In general terms, the same basic comparison can be made between artificial and natural materials in the home. While there is something utterly forlorn about aged synthetics, the patina of old wood or weathered stone flags is both uplifting and reassuring.

Lurking behind this aesthetic preference is the desire for continuity. This is not merely the continuity of tradition, the satisfaction of using materials that have been employed for thousands of years, but a deeper sense of connection with nature itself. We can see the living source of wood in the pattern of grain on a table top, but who, besides a petrochemical technician, could name the

Bold, luminous colour across a large expanse of wall can best be achieved by applying a much-diluted colourwash of water-based emulsion (latex), tinted with artist's pigment. Applied with generous brush strokes over a white ground, the result will be an informal, totally textured finish.

polymers in melamine? Industrial production, particularly on the scale and of the complexity it has attained in the postwar years, has a distancing effect, severing all kinds of links which have been woven into human society over many centuries. Enthusiasm for natural products can be seen as a reflection of our desire to re-forge these links. Nostalgia may be a suspect emotion, but it is

far from new. Ever since the Industrial Revolution there have been concerted efforts to preserve connections both with nature itself and with the traditional crafts and skills implied in the use of natural materials. William Morris and his followers in the Arts and Crafts Movement harked back to pre-Renaissance days to identify with the artisanship of craftsmen working on the great medieval cathedrals. The Middle Ages was the starting point for Morris's revival of all types of craft, from the art of making stained glass windows to the process of extracting natural dyes from vegetable matter. The fact that the craft aesthetic still flourishes today owes much to his efforts, as does the fact that we have learned to revere old farmhouse kitchens as much as grand state rooms.

It is easy to poke fun at the idea of sophisticated people yearning for the simple life. But it is a yearning that just will not go away. Many people deliberately seek to satisfy it at least once a year when they go away on holiday. Country cottages, beach huts or Greek island villas all offer elemental settings that help to refresh the spirits. If we go to such lengths, and distances, to enjoy the revitalizing benefits of nature, why shouldn't we endeavour to make our everyday surroundings more natural themselves?

At the end of the twentieth century the strongest argument in favour of natural decorating must be ecological. Natural materials, which ultimately return to the earth, which are renewable and sustainable, are self-evidently

Myriad shades of white, ranging from aged, dirty white to cream, taupe and biscuit, show how restful 'no colour' can be.

better in the long run than materials that pollute, deplete precious resources and create unacceptable residues as a consequence of their production. We do not know the real long-term health effects of many of the chemicals and additives that routinely permeate our homes, but the damage they have already caused to the environment as a whole cannot be disputed.

Natural decorating should not be seen as a way of urging an impossibly 'green' lifestyle. Houses can only be thoroughly ecological when they are designed and built with that specific intention. For most of us, it is not an either/or issue, rather an accumulative process by which we gradually question the relevance and value of synthetic substitutes for the real thing. Just as public concern with healthier eating has prompted food manufacturers to remove unnecessary additives and alter production methods, it is likely that an

This simple seaside hut, with its weatherbeaten timbers, nestles in an uncluttered landscape where land meets sea. Strident colours gently faded by the elements, basic lighting and ultra-simple furnishings all help to create an atmosphere of contemplation and relaxation.

Pebbles are often inlaid into walls and floors where the indigenous stonework is less than strong. A stone 'walkway' eases pressure on bare feet and provides comfortable access to both the seating and the fireplace. Cochineal-coloured plaster, recessed stone alcoves and exposed timbers evoke images of a cave dwelling.

increasing awareness of the drawbacks of artificial materials, which promise so much but deliver so little, will foster a return to the natural basics that have served so well for many centuries.

Sources of inspiration

Natural decorating embraces a whole family of linked approaches, deriving from vernacular traditions as well as contemporary styles.

One aspect of natural decorating takes the vibrancy and vitality of ethnic artefacts and craftwork as a point of departure. Dhurries from India, batik from Indonesia, South American appliqué, printed African cloths, glowing Mexican ceramics, woven rattan and wicker are no longer regarded as the exotic souvenirs of a global trek, but the common stock-in-trade purveyed in many high street shops. The expanding network of communications with far-flung corners of the world has led to a renewed appreciation of indigenous skills, and natural materials and colourings. Even if the vernacular is not our own, we can still appreciate the direct relationship between maker and product, the subtle variations from piece to piece and the unselfconscious artistry of such handiwork.

Another source of influence comes from the calm spaces of the traditional Japanese house and garden. When Japan reopened trading links with the West in the mid-nineteenth century, the effect on European artists, designers and architects was electrifying. On the popular level, the cult of Japan was rapidly translated into the superficial: peacock feathers and fans, Japanese-style porcelain and latticed or lacquered furniture were instantly fashionable. But the Japanese aesthetic had a more profound and lasting influence on the designers of the Arts and Crafts Movement, who sought to challenge the density, clutter and artificiality of Victorian decorating. The traditional Japanese house seemed to offer the perfect balance between art and nature, decoration and simplicity.

A century later, the Japanese aesthetic is valued for very much the same reasons. Nature is central to the idea of the Japanese house, both in its symbolism and in its use of materials. Tatami, floor mats of woven straw edged with linen, provide the module for room size; their slightly springy surface cushions the rough wood floor. Sliding screens covered in thick paper provide internal divisions and can be pushed back to open small rooms into one large space. A small recess, or tokonoma, serves as a place for the display of art objects or flowers. Closets house clothing, rolls of bedding and other household articles, stowed away when not in use in order to leave the floor space clear. The severe formality is complemented by an ever-present sense of nature. Wooden support posts and beams may be left in a natural state, sometimes with the bark intact; windows may be screened with mulberry paper shoji, doorways with bamboo bead curtains, elegantly fusing structure, decoration and material. Outdoors, the formal arrangement of rocks,

The view is not the only natural element of this outdoor haven. Resist-dyed cotton draped on a bamboo chair blends harmoniously with the smooth, sunbleached timber of a decked balcony.

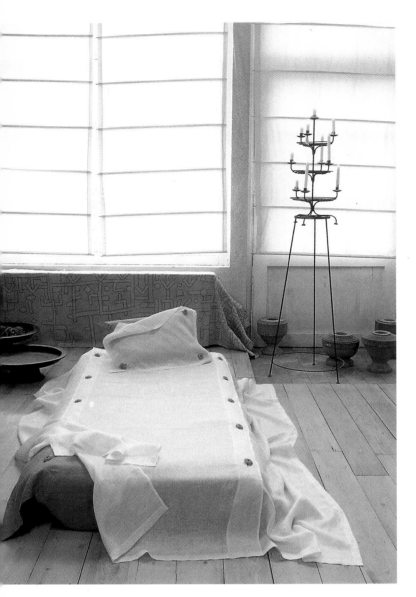

raked gravel, water, lanterns, dwarf trees and shrubs summarizes the elemental forces of nature.

Western traditions, enshrined in log cabins, cob houses, tithe barns and thatched cottages, provide another powerful source of influence. Whether such traditions are expressed in the simplicity of a Shaker interior or the honest exposure of brick, stone or timber in an old farmhouse, an appreciation of natural elements often lurks behind our absorbing interest in the rural past.

But natural decorating need not imply an exotic or backward-looking approach. Modern design, with its well-worn credo 'less is more', has concentrated attention on the structural realities of the interior, the direct expression of materials, the

A variation on the Japanese theme of low-level living has been applied here using hessian (burlap) and linen bedding, thrown clay pots and draped furniture. The windows are covered with white sheeting to form sheer blinds (shades).

play of light and the use of colour, texture and pattern without recourse to imitation or pastiche. Natural materials and finishes fit well into this type of aesthetic, offering their own inbuilt interest and character.

On an even more basic level, the impulse for natural decorating can arise simply from an affection for landscape. Stuck in traffic, cocooned in office blocks or housed in uniform city streets, the thirst for natural surroundings becomes ever more acute. The elements with which we surround ourselves can be alienating – or not. By acting as a reminder of the natural world, prosaic mementoes such as shells, beach stones and driftwood, and fundamental qualities such as the grain of floorboards and *freshness of cotton, soothe the senses and serve to redress the balance.*

Creating a natural scheme

Natural decorating cannot really be reduced to a neat formula; there are as many ways of creating the look as there are reasons for doing so. Natural decorating is often identified with the calm neutrality of white on white, or the reticent combination of

pale woods, unbleached natural fibres, stone and matting. This interpretation turns a room into a refuge, a retreat from the clamour of colour and sensation that accompanies everyday life. The more frenetic and pressured our lives become, the more urgent our need for peaceful, comfortable surroundings where we can refresh our spirits and recover a sense of equilibrium.

Banishing clutter and colour from a room, however, will not necessarily result in a sense of Zen-like calm. Achieving this kind of simplicity is not as straightforward as merely paring away superfluous detail: near-empty rooms can be bland and featureless if you do not pay attention to scale, texture, contrast and, surprisingly enough, colour.

A decorative scheme which is based on the use of white or neutral tones needs to be composed as carefully as one which is teeming with colour and pattern. To begin with, you cannot assume that all whites are the same. The pure unadulterated white of whitewash, for example, will tend to make other less pure whites look dirty by comparison. Different whites, different textures and different surfaces will all reflect light in their own ways: some will look shiny and glossy, others matt, others more textured. To create a harmonious neutral background, it is necessary to assemble samples of the various textures and finishes and assess combinations that will work together successfully. The same basic approach also holds true for neutral tones in the spectrum from cream to

Scrupulously bare yet rich in texture, this traditional Japanese house shows how natural materials used in juxtaposition create their own harmony and interest without needing expensive pieces of furniture to frame the view. Black bound-edged sisal mats echo the walls, creating a fretwork cocoon relieved only by the windows, a rice-paper screen and paper lampshade.

light brown – the sandy, grey or biscuit shades prevalent in natural unfinished wood, fabric and stone. Some tints may be warmer, some cooler, and not all will work together sympathetically.

Textural contrast can go a long way to distract from tonal differences. Many successful rooms have been created using closely related tones and textures, but the risk of a rather numbing uniformity is high. Provided smooth is counterpoised with rough, matt with glossy, the danger of blandness recedes.

Another variable is scale. In rooms where nothing is highly coloured or patterned, emphasis can come from juxtaposing small areas of detail with the outsize. Large sofas conceal their bulk under white loose (slip) covers; displays of twigs or branches add theatricality to muted surroundings. You can have fun with proportional tricks in rooms that otherwise pull their punches.

But natural decorating does not necessarily imply avoidance of strong colour. There is nothing subdued about nature, nor do natural pigments and materials offer a limited palette of discreet neutral shades. Forest green, poppy red, ochre and indigo are every bit as natural in derivation and mood as more delicate tones. Provided the sources of such colours are natural in themselves, colour mixing is not a problem. As William Morris's experiments with natural dyes confirmed, you can combine any number of such colours without stridency. And as far as natural dyes are concerned, these shades fade in unison with each other, retaining their innate balance even when worn. The same is not true of more synthetic shades. If you are looking for a more colourful version of natural decorating, the combinations will more or less take care of themselves.

With the emphasis on the colour, pattern and texture of materials, there is less need for clutter in the interior. Natural ingredients seem to need room to breathe. This does not rule out a sense of liveliness or variety. One of the best lessons that can be learned from the natural world is its essential changefulness, and responding to nature means keeping in touch with seasonal alterations in light, mood and growth that can be observed in the landscape. Changing displays and furnishings to reflect the atmosphere of different times of the year is an obvious way of keeping interiors alive.

The combination of white bargeboarding, sunbleached and weatherbeaten wooden tables, and muted ochre and terracotta soft furnishings allows the light to surge through the windows and bounce off the surfaces of this timbered house. An abundance of daylight brings the outside in.

WALLS

WALLS

A thin yellow ochre wash over raw plaster walls creates a pleasantly textured backdrop for colourful painted furniture and exposed roof timbers. The classic colour combination of sunshine yellow and deep green makes for a restful, welcoming room (ABOVE).

The robust integrity of an exposed brick wall provides a simple, timeworn starting point for a sparse decorative scheme in this sculptor's home (RIGHT).

Walls enclose and demarcate space; they literally shape our surroundings. Collectively, walls amount to the largest surface area in any room whatever its dimensions: for this reason alone, decorative choices must inevitably start here. Whether you paint, paper or panel, the treatment you adopt becomes a room's signature note, the basis for the orchestration of fittings and furnishings that follows.

In early or primitive dwellings, walls are naturally expressive elements. The rugged rustication of thick stone walls in ancient fortified manors and castles has a visible integrity, no less direct than the corrugated surface of a log cabin's interlocking timbers or the smooth baked earth of an adobe hut. The structural function of such walls can be read equally from inside the building as from outside. But in more complex or sophisticated dwellings, where walls are often covered by a series of applied finishes obscuring the structural realities beneath, the material dimension may be all but lost.

Natural wall finishes represent an attempt to restore the connection. In some cases, such a strategy may amount simply to respecting what is already there. Areas of exposed brickwork or stone in old cottages, farmhouses and reclaimed industrial warehouses, can be relished for the rhythmic and textural contrast they provide; when left in as unfinished a state as possible, they also serve to recall the wall's functional purpose. In the same way, the mellow frescoed quality of bare plaster has become an increasingly popular way of adding a homely depth and character to an interior.

Unlike floors or other surfaces with which we necessarily have direct physical contact, we tend not to go about touching walls. Nevertheless, wall finishes that supply little textural interest can impoverish our experience of living spaces. Utterly bland backgrounds may be safe and uncontroversial but their extreme reticence can often undermine any attempt to give a room a feeling of vitality and atmosphere. From the faintest whisper of whitewash over rough plaster to robust matchboard cladding, natural wall treatments have a certain tactile quality that provides an added dimension.

If natural finishes bring texture to the fore, tonality is an equally important factor. Pale colours are open and expansive, accentuating the effect of natural light. Dark or intense tones draw you into a cosy hospitable circle. Standard decorating advice generally recommends that rooms which do not

A neutral, unadorned floor perfectly complements the raw plaster walls in a simple yet sophisticated kitchen. The warm richness of undecorated pink plaster casts an inviting glow over the pale wood table and chairs. A glass panelled door and window of similar proportions are left bare, to allow light to flood in and to echo the clean, functional lines of the room.

receive much direct light should be decorated in lighter tones to redress the balance; in fact, if the aspect of a room is irredeemably poor, a light-toned background will simply look dingy and insipid. In such circumstances, deep, rich or mellow tones work infinitely better and turn an inherent drawback into a positive asset. Conversely, the sunnier the room, the lighter the

decoration can be. White, sun-drenched walls become a radiant extension of a brilliant outlook.

Within the essentially neutral palette of natural materials, there is a surprisingly wide, if subtle, variety of different shades, but natural decorating does not exclude a more forthright use of colour. When it comes to promoting a link with nature, colour provides an instant short cut of association, from the seashore shades of misty blue, grey-green and sand, to rich earthy ochres and terracottas.

Paint

Paint is the most straightforward of all wall treatments, offering an affordable, virtually instant transformation of any surface. If you are concerned solely with achieving a 'natural look', regardless of ecological or historical credentials, modern paint ranges offer a staggeringly broad choice of colour and finish. Most of us are familiar with the alternatives of emulsion (latex), gloss and eggshell (lustre) paint, and their recommended applications. A friendly supplier and a little perseverance together with a willingness to experiment with sample pots, will enable most enthusiastic home decorators to come up with an appropriately 'natural' shade.

Specialist paint ranges that are themed around historical or vernacular decorating traditions take the hard work out of selection. While there may be significantly fewer colours available, the palette as a whole will have been carefully designed so that colours work well together, making the process of choice much less daunting. In fact, the multiplicity of shades available from major paint manufacturers, enshrined in those bewildering colour cards, can be misleading. Many of the variables are simply versions of a single core shade, darkened or lightened by degrees.

'Natural' colours can be selected by making a comparison with the type of material you wish to evoke. Traditionally, interior surfaces were often painted to recall the quality of the underlying material. In other words, woodwork was painted to look 'woody', walls to look like stone or something similar. Without resorting to the type of wholesale fakery

implied by wood graining, marbling or other such faux finishes, you can opt for any of the subtle neutral shades from ivory to biscuit, stone to slate grey, buff to ochre, and achieve a background which complements natural finishes and furnishings in a discreet, understated way. At its simplest, a natural paint finish may be natural only in the sense of sympathetic colour choice.

Modern paints, like other artificial materials, have been developed to fulfil certain specific requirements, among which are quick drying times, washable and resilient surfaces, and colour consistency with predictable and repeatable colour matching. These were not insignificant advantages a couple of generations ago, when the alternative was a patchy or streaky finish, laborious application and an appreciable shift in colour from batch to batch. In previous centuries, householders had to rely on the skill of professional house painters to achieve desired results. We may like to imagine that such trades people were the purveyors of an arcane skill, but the reality, at a general level, was probably very different. In 1883, a brochure produced for Morris and Co. railed against the 'dirty no-colours' then standard in the repertoire of domestic house-painters: 'The use of positive colour is very difficult, and house-painters are peculiarly ignorant of it. Their incapacity may have led to the use of the dull, gray, even dirty shades, which have become so general since house decoration began to interest educated people...'.

Morris was especially keen to disassociate himself from 'greenery-yallery', the subdued, muddy colour which was the height of fashion in late Victorian artistic circles. Its tonal impurity was not dissimilar to 'drab', an appropriately named serviceable shade,

A vivid, revitalizing cerulean blue colourwash, lightly applied over bare plaster, creates a Mediterranean-style shower area. A single tile placed in the wall recess is echoed in a simple mural above the window.

created by mixing the dregs of all the other paint colours used elsewhere in the house to make a suitably utilitarian shade for kitchens, pantries and below-stairs rooms. 'Drab', a 'dirty no-colour' if ever there was one, was ideal for disguising the routine discoloration of walls by the smoky fumes emitted by gas jets, kitchen ranges and coal fires.

However, those decorators who are acquainted with the subtlety of traditional paints such as distemper, limewash and milk paint remind us that coating a wall with modern synthetic paint is equivalent to applying a thin skin of plastic to the surface. It may not be immediately obvious to those of us who have no point of comparison, but the drawbacks of such finishes are akin to those of any other synthetic material: poor ageing, little depth and characterless colours. In addition to these aesthetic disadvantages, environmentalists have alerted us to the

potential toxicity of many of the ingredients involved in the manufacture of synthetic paint. Over a period of time, such pollutants 'out-gas' from painted surfaces, impregnating the atmosphere with potentially hazardous chemicals.

All paint consists of a pigment, which gives colour and body, suspended in a medium (normally water or oil). In the past, linseed oil and natural resins were used as paint media; but these have been largely replaced in the postwar period by petrochemical substitutes which are largely responsible for synthetic paint's polluting effect. Some types of paint also include additives such as fungicides and insecticides. Lead was once a common additive but its use in paint is now banned in Britain and the United States.

In the quest for authenticity 'natural' can never be taken as entirely synonymous with 'harmless'. In certain remote parts of the world colouring remains as simple as grinding a handful of the nearest clay, mixing it into a paste with water and scrubbing it onto the wall. Our ancestors, however, made use of such 'natural' pigments as red lead oxide, arsenic, mercury and copper manganese, among others – highly toxic ingredients, the use of which is sensibly now prohibited. Natural pigments today, derived largely from mineral and earth deposits, are mercifully not authentic to that degree. Plants are also a good source of natural colour, and pigments derived from roots, flowers, stems and leaves are being reintroduced.

For thorough-going devotees of natural decorating, organic pigments and paints may well provide the best solution. Colours range from bright, clear shades to the earthier vegetable tones beloved of the heritage lobby. Their common ingredients – citrus extracts, chalk, pine resin and linseed oil – are in no way deleterious to health and

Adobe-style exterior walls built from mud and sun-baked clay have been further decorated with an application of coloured limewash and a whitewash decorative border around the door (ABOVE LEFT).

Floor-to-ceiling tongue-and-groove boarding and a floor covered with seagrass matting contribute to a subdued and uncomplicated country home. Colour is used to create a dado (chair) rail and break up the wall space in hallway and living room (RIGHT).

well-being and their only disadvantage is a relatively slow drying time, which allows the skin of the paint to accommodate itself to the underlying material. Organic paints, even oil-based varieties, have the added advantage of permitting the wall to breathe. Unlike modern synthetic paints, which seal the wall under immutable impermeable layers, organic paints seep into the base material and permit natural ventilation to take place. Another extremely persuasive argument for choosing organic paints is their biodegradability. Modern paint manufacture creates ninety per cent wastage, which is utterly unrecyclable; residues are typically disposed of in huge land dumps. Organic paint, on the other hand, can be completely recycled.

Whichever type of paint you choose, the finish can be enhanced by adopting traditional methods of application that result in a textured, broken finish. Broken colour techniques, or what are commonly known as 'paint effects', have hurtled in and out of fashion at an alarming rate over the last decade. Today, the more sumptuous, overtly contrived finishes, simulating fabric-hung or marble-clad walls have practically disappeared along with a tolerance for such obvious displays of conspicuous consumption. Nevertheless, the intention behind such methods, to introduce textural dimension and depth, remains relevant. There is nothing wrong with matt, evenly painted colour on the wall; in many situations, such finishes provide an ideal backdrop. But broken colour techniques can be allied to the natural aesthetic to create a sense of informality and ruggedness.

Part of the charm of natural pigments is their soft, slightly patchy look. Like other natural materials, such finishes age well, fading gently in the sunlight.

Applying successive layers of thinly diluted water-based paint, so that brushmarks remain visible, is another way of creating a lively surface. Rubbing paint onto the wall with a cloth also avoids the mechanical look of a paint-rollered finish. Broken colour effects generally work best if you use two or more closely related shades – a base coat covered with a broken finish a tone lighter or darker. Sand added to oil-based paint creates an interesting granular finish that resembles stone, while freehand chevrons or squiggles trimming the margins of a wall introduce a more ethnic effect.

White is the classic contemporary background, the ultimate neutral. White paint washed over brick, tongue-and-groove panelling or rough plaster has a straightforward simplicity. The origin of white as a positive element in domestic decoration dates back to the nineteenth century. William Morris and his followers in the Arts and Crafts Movement shocked contemporary Victorian society by their advocacy of plain white walls and woodwork. At that time, humble whitewash was a standard treatment for outbuildings, privies or cowsheds: painting a drawing room white was tantamount to leaving it unfinished. Designers of the Arts and Crafts Movement, who urged an honest use of materials, were the first to view white in a favourable way. 'White is perfectly neutral; it is a perfect foil for most colours, and by judicious toning may be assimilated with any,' stated the Morris and Co. brochure of 1883, and William Morris recommended 'honest whitewash...on which sun and shadow play so pleasantly' as an alternative to tapestry, fresco or mosaic should these prove too expensive.

Morris held very decided opinions on the correct way of carrying out

These exterior walls benefit from a thin veil of whitewash which falls short of a door surround and finishes at dado (chair rail) height to give the impression of a decorative border (LEFT).

Occasionally, old walls stripped of myriad layers of wallpaper yield original painted decoration. Enhanced with a new terrazzo skirting and wooden floor, this crumbling paintwork provides a delightful multi-textured backdrop (ABOVE).

Walls colourwashed to dado (chair rail) height can create a sense of architectural symmetry. Extra definition comes from painted woodwork, such as door frames and window reveals, picked out in a deeper tone.

whitewashing. Achieving the 'right' white is no less of a vexing issue today. Modern white can be a harsh, chilly shade, owing to the blue tint manufacturers add to achieve a look of 'brilliance'. Plain trade white, widely available from specialist paint suppliers, is softer and mellows with age. For those who prefer a more ambiguous shade, plain white can be 'dirtied' a little by adding a dollop or two of a warmer off-white, just enough to take the edge off the freshness of new paintwork.

The traditional white paints, limewash and distemper, are much valued for their matt, chalky texture. You can make up these paints today to their original recipes with ingredients available from specialist suppliers, but their use in the interior is necessarily somewhat limited (see page 36). Distemper is chemically incompatible with modern paints and

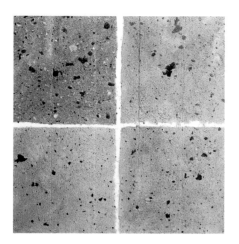

claustrophobia in formal dining rooms. However, covering a wall with paper is a perfectly natural approach to decorating, and offers a wide range of exciting possibilities for achieving lively textured effects.

There has never been a better time for investigating the potential of paper. There is a huge variety of recycled or handmade papers available in art suppliers and ethnic emporia, papers that offer delightfully nubbly surfaces flecked with colour or embedded with shreds of grass, petals or stalks. Japanese rush or grass papers, with their ribbed, slubbed surface, or papers made of even more exotic materials, such as those from Bangladesh made of recycled water hyacinth, are usually affordable enough to make the prospect of covering at least a small room practicable. These papers are generally sold as wrapping paper, and chiefly come in sizes scaled for that purpose, although larger sheets are becoming increasingly available.

Virtually any type of paper, provided it is not too fragile, can be pasted up on the wall just like conventional wallpaper. (Incidentally, some manufacturers of organic paints and finishes also produce organic wallpaper paste.) Recycled or handmade papers tend to come with wavy or deckled edges which can be trimmed if you are keen to achieve a seamless effect. Otherwise, smaller squares of paper can be pasted up with a little margin left around each one; the effect is astonishingly reminiscent of tiling. The random speckling of handmade paper has an uncanny resemblance to the aggregate mottling of terrazzo. You can exploit this similarity by papering sections of the wall that might otherwise be tiled – the inside of a window reveal, for example. Self-contained areas, such as the alcoves flanking a chimney breast, are other

must be applied over fresh plaster, or a surface that has been completely stripped of previous finishes, otherwise it will flake off. Limewash is extremely caustic and must be handled with care.

Paper

Wallpaper often conjures up images of quaint floral sprigs smothering the walls of back bedrooms, or busy, rather stuffy prints inducing a faint sense of

Handmade paper in subtle colours and textures can be used instead of wall tiles. Bold squares, pasted onto the wall with a narrow margin around each square, achieve a 'tiled' chequerboard effect (TOP).

Areas such as the space beneath a stairway, or the alcoves flanking a chimney, lend themselves to papered decoration. In this entrance hall a papered wall echoes the flooring. (ABOVE).

Wooden panelling on ceiling and walls in a dining room creates a warm sense of enclosure and an inviting atmosphere for intimate entertaining (ABOVE).

This cool living room requires no adornment other than a casual collection of pine cones and rough clay pots, whose rich texture echoes the rough-with-smooth finish of a cane chair and the tile-hung walls (RIGHT).

good locations for this type of treatment if you do not wish to paper an entire wall or room.

Ordinary brown wrapping paper, available in economical rolls, has its own merits as a natural surface. You can choose which side to expose; one side is normally smooth, the other has a more obvious nap. Wrapping paper – or lining paper for that matter – makes a good base for stencilled designs. The decorative pedigree of this approach is a good one: Charles Rennie Mackintosh favoured coarse brown wrapping paper as a wall treatment for dining rooms, where its sombre yet neutral tone complemented the glitter of glass and silver on the table. In the dining room of his own house, Mackintosh stencilled abstract, organically inspired shapes onto a brown paper background, highlighted with small dabs of silver, painted freehand.

Natural fibres, such as woven raffia or hessian (burlap), are also available in a paper-backed form for more conventional paper hanging. Trimming the joins with wooden moulding stained black suggests the refined aesthetic of the traditional Japanese house.

Papered walls can be coated with water-based varnish to seal the surface, but be sure that the varnish you choose does not yellow with age, unless you positively welcome that effect. Alternatively, they can be painted, although many papers are so intrinsically beautiful that it would be a shame to cover them up.

Panelling

Lining a room in wood generally provokes an immediate and favourable response: wood is warm, homely and somehow reassuring. Panelling can disguise a poor underlying surface and complement or adjust architectural proportions. The innate rhythm of planks or panels is extremely satisfying in itself and makes any room instantly more human in scale. The warmth is more than apparent: wood is an effective insulator, not only against the cold but also against sound.

Unless you live in rather grand surroundings, any original panelling in your house is probably made of softwood. Panelled shutter housings or window reveals in Victorian houses, for example, are largely made of pine. Such surfaces were always painted, since cheap, resinous softwoods were never considered attractive enough to be left exposed. You can retain the impression of woodiness and grain by applying wood stain (available in colours as well as 'woody' shades); alternatively, water-based or emulsion paint provides a matt finish that allows a little of the graininess to show through. Applying several thin layers, rubbed well down with sandpaper between coats, results in a gently distressed or aged surface. Traditionally, wooden surfaces were painted with oil-based paints, but these sleek finishes obliterate rather than reveal the underlying material. If you wish to leave the wood exposed after stripping, all you need to apply is a light coat of linseed oil or beeswax.

Tongue-and-groove boarding – or 'matchboarding' – has a rather different aesthetic, but one that is no less evocative or pleasing. Think of snug ship's cabins and the enveloping quality of simple planked panelling is instantly apparent. Traditionally, tongue-and-groove boarding is applied to the side of bathtubs, or up to dado level in bathrooms or hallways where it provides a robust, waterproof surface when painted. But it is much more versatile than that. In the absence of other architectural detail, tongue-and-groove

boarding fixed solely to the ceiling can warm and enliven an otherwise featureless room, creating a sense of enclosure. In a living area, white-painted or colourwashed boarding looks faintly nautical. It can be fixed either vertically or horizontally.

Panelling can also be constructed from reclaimed timber or weathered wood if you would like a more overtly rustic effect. Salvage yards are often a good source of ingredients such as pieces of old wall panelling or panels from chests or doors, which can be reworked into a new format. New panelling should be made of wood derived from indigenous sources or managed plantations.

Plaster

Raw plaster is one of the more unlikely decorating trends of recent years; or if not real raw plaster, at least the effect of it. The reasons for this are fairly obvious. Anyone who has ever seen untreated plasterwork cannot fail to respond to its warm, mellow tones, reminiscent of antique frescoed walls. It offers an appealingly unfinished surface, mottled in soft tones of terracotta and displaying the forthright honesty of a material exposed for what it is. As well as the standard pinkish variety, plaster is also available in shades of white or grey, which can be equally handsome.

Plaster is an excellent natural material. As an interior finish, it breathes well. If you are ecologically minded, avoid covering plasterwork with an impermeable finish, such as synthetic oil-based paints or vinyl wallpaper.

There is no real reason why plasterwork cannot simply be left in its natural state, without any subsequent treatment. The sole disadvantage of doing so is that the surface can become a little powdery and dusty. One remedy is

No danger of feeling landlocked in this bold grotto with its dense mosaic of seashells and glass fragments inlaid in concrete. Witty seating is provided in the form of a conch-shaped chair (ABOVE).

The broken surfaces of translucent rose-washed walls and whitewashed floorboards, the clever combination of plain materials and varied textures, and bold, simple shapes make this the epitome of a sleek but simple natural room (LEFT).

to seal the surface by rubbing in a thin coating of wax or sealant, but this also tends to darken the colour. To counteract the effect, you can add lighter tints to the sealant.

You can also manipulate the texture of plaster by rubbing fine metallic chips, sawdust or straw into the surface before it has dried. In the same way, wet plaster can be lightly scored or embedded with a pattern of small shells or pebbles for a tribal look.

Tiles

The charming irregularity of handmade tiles provides an instant connection to the earth. Terracotta (literally fired earth) is only one of a number of types of tile that can be used to enrich and protect interior surfaces. Ceramic tiles and mosaic come in a brilliant palette of colours and finishes to lend a luminous quality to walls. Tiles are available in a variety of sizes, glazed or unglazed, plain or decorative. (Unglazed wall tiles used as splashbacks in kitchens and bathrooms must be sealed.)

Although handmade tiles are the most expensive, they are also the most beautiful. Tiles that are individually glazed have a remarkable vitality en masse, which is entirely lacking in the rather soulless machine-made versions. Traditional Provençal tiles, in warm ochres, earthy reds and greens, make an exuberant yet homely backdrop on kitchen walls.

Mosaic provides the opportunity to create intricately decorative designs or pictures literally set into the fabric of the wall. Colours range from muted matt shades of grey-greens and blues to searing primaries and shimmering metallics. Simple designs are not outside the scope of the amateur, but for large-scale pictorial panels it is better to commission a mosaic artist.

This colourful splashback, made from traditional, mismatching majolica tiles from the southern Mediterranean, has a pleasing irregular sheen which provides a sympathetic contrast to the roughly hewn stone sink.

WHITE ON WHITE

A room decorated in various shades of white is a decorating classic. This treatment is especially effective in rooms where natural light can be enhanced to provide a neutral, and timeless, backdrop for furniture and furnishings.

Three shades of white painted on a wall show just how wide the range of 'white' paint can be. The ubiquitous brilliant white emulsion (latex), produced by every paint manufacturer, is rarely the best white to choose, especially in a northern climate, as it casts a bluish glare which is uninviting. Much more atmospheric are the slightly 'dirty' whites produced by traditional distemper (or whitewash). Artists' tinting pigments or oils can be added to paint to lend warmth to white: try a dash of burnt sienna or yellow ochre.

DISTEMPER WASH
Commercially produced, oil-based 'hard' distemper is once again available from specialist paint suppliers (see pages 141–2). Traditional distemper, however, characterized by a soft, matt, powdery finish, is made from a base of whiting or chalk, mixed with water and bound with hot size glue. This 'soft' distemper is really suitable only for replenishing original cornice-work in older houses, while 'hard' distemper can be used on all interior walls.

The attractive chalky finish of soft distemper allows walls to breathe, but it is less permanent than emulsion paint and is susceptible to damp. An important point to remember is that once you have used distemper on walls you cannot apply ordinary emulsion on top of it as it will simply peel off.

PREPARATION
You should only make up the distemper once you have prepared your walls for decorating, since it is best used as soon as it is made up. It will only keep for a day or so in an airtight container in the refrigerator.

MATERIALS
This quantity will make approximately 5 lits (1 gall) of distemper:
5lit (1 gall) bucket of water
20k (44lbs) whiting
1.5 lits (2½ pts) hot size glue (made up according to manufacturer's instructions and kept warm in a bain-marie)

METHOD
1 Sift the whiting into the bucket until a small amount of powder appears above the surface. Leave the mixture overnight, then pour off the excess water. Stir in the hot glue before using.

2 To colour the distemper, you should mix about ½k (1lb) of the tinting pigment with water until it forms a paste, then add it to the paint.

FLAT-OIL GLAZE
There are other ways of producing a similar effect using readily available materials, for example, flat-oil glaze. Flat-oil paint can be found in most specialist paint shops and is used on walls by professional decorators to achieve a silky smooth finish. Water it down considerably – about 2 parts paint to 8 parts water – and apply it over a ground of water-based white emulsion. The result is a matt, transparent sheen.

RECYCLING PAPER

Natural papers have a long tradition in both Eastern and Western cultures. Applied to wall surfaces, their subtle colours and natural textures make them an ideal decorating medium. Recycling paper is environmentally friendly and the end results can look quite stunning. Most paper can be recycled, but the strongest fibres are contained in computer paper, newspaper, gift-wrapping paper and Manilla envelopes.

To make A4 (295 x 210mm/8½ x 11¾in) sheets for use as wallpaper, you will need a mould and deckle (see right). Do not use any tools that might rust and cause small brown spots, or 'foxing', to appear. The addition of plant materials, such as bluebells, cherry blossom, or boiled and sieved leeks or rhubarb, will enhance both the texture and the colour of the finished paper.

MOULD AND DECKLE

4 pieces of wood 2 x 3cm (¾ x 1⅛in), 20cm (8in) long
4 pieces of wood 2 x 3cm (¾ x 1⅛in), 15cm (6in) long
Brass or aluminum mesh with 5-10 holes per sq cm (30–65 holes per sq in), or fabric mesh 10–15 holes per sq cm (65–90 per sq in)
Panel pins
8 flat L-shaped braces
Screws

PREPARATION

The frames of the mould and deckle can also be made by recycling old picture frames: two frames 20 x 15cm (8 x 6in) would be ideal. Whether using this method or constructing your own frame, choose wood that is not too knotted or twisted as this will effect the end result: smooth pine is the best option. Remove any paint or varnish from wooden frames and strengthen any glued joints using rustproof screws or nails. The coarser the screen, the coarser the paper produced; finer screens will produce a more smoothly textured surface.

METHOD

1 To make the mould, lay out the four pieces of wood – two measuring 20cm (8in) long and two measuring 15cm (6in) – to form a rectangle. Pin the joints together with panel pins and then strengthen them with L-shaped braces. Repeat the whole process to make the deckle.

2 Place a sheet of mesh over the mould and attach it using brass nails or copper staples.

3 The finished mould and deckle.

4 It is on the mould that the sheet of paper is formed.

1

2

3

4

PAPER-MAKING

Different types of paper will produce different effects. Computer paper is ideal as it has long, strong fibres. Standard newspaper will turn grey when pulped and is best used in combination with other papers. Pink newspaper will turn brown when dry. Paper bags or envelopes can also be used.

MATERIALS FOR PAPER-MAKING

Recyclable paper of your choice
Large bowl, 15cm (6in) minimum
    depth, and large enough to hold the
    mould and deckle with ease
Blender or food processor with 1lit
    (1¾pt) capacity
2 plastic buckets
Sponge
Sieve or colander
Hand whisk
Rolling pin
Plastic bowls for excess pulp
Palette knife

PREPARING THE PULP

1 Remove any remnants of staples, glue or other foreign matter from your paper.

2 Tear the paper into 3cm (1¼in) squares and soak in water overnight or up to a week to break it down further. Alternatively, you can pour boiling water over the paper and leave for a couple of hours.

3 Liquidize the soaked paper a batch at a time. Try 10-15 pieces of paper for each ¾lit (1⅓ pts) to begin with. Liquidize for about 15 seconds. If lumps are still present, repeat the process. You are aiming for a smooth, creamy consistency.

4 To form a sheet of paper, fill the bowl with pulp so that the mould and deckle can be easily immersed in it. Stir the pulp quickly by hand or with a whisk.

MAKING PAPER SHEETS

1 Place the deckle over the mould, against the mesh, and hold them together. Stand both mould and deckle vertically in the far side of the bowl.

2 Tilt them as smoothly and slowly as possible into a horizontal position, gently pulling the frames forwards until they are thoroughly immersed, then upwards so that they come out of the pulp still in a horizontal position. As you lift the mould and deckle out, the suction on the mesh causes the fibres to adhere to it; the force can be quite strong.

3 With the mould and deckle still horizontal, shake them from side to side and front to back. Hold the mould and deckle above the bowl, slightly tilted to get rid of any excess water from the pulp.

DRYING THE PAPER

Place the mould and deckle on a flat surface. Carefully remove the deckle from the mould so that no drips fall onto the pulp that is on the mesh. Any drips that do fall will cause holes to appear in the paper.

To dry the paper, leave the mould to stand on a pad of newspaper, pulp side up. The pad will need renewing a few times before the sheet is dry. When most of the excess water has drained away you can tilt the mould. Prop it up against a wall or cupboard to finish drying. When the paper has completely dried out, remove it from the mould with a palette knife as if removing a cake from a baking tin, gently easing the sheet of paper away from the mesh.

FADED FRESCO

1

2

3

4

Before rushing to paint over the natural pink or grey tones of a newly plastered or stripped wall, try instead to enhance what is already there. The scumbled finish of an old faded fresco is a relatively simple technique to emulate. Once you have achieved the desired shade, you can embellish the wall further by painting on a few fresco motifs such as fruit, leaves or geometric patterns, and then ageing them as in steps 3 and 4.

MATERIALS

2 shades of dusky pink water-based
     emulsion (latex) paint (2.5 lits/½ gall
     covers about 25 sq m/82 sq ft)
Water for thinning
2 paintbrushes (10cm/4in, 5cm/2in)
Fine-grade sandpaper
2 buckets
Soft cloth for buffing

PREPARATION

If applying paint to new plaster, make sure the plaster has dried out completely. If applying it to a wall stripped of wallpaper, ensure that all traces of paper and paste are removed before sanding gently to smooth the surface. Fill any holes with a proprietary filler and sand again. The surface does not have to be a uniform colour since you will be applying a light wash of paint to it. The finished effect to aim for is one of broken colour.

METHOD

1 Mix together two shades of dusky pink water-based emulsion in a bucket until you have the desired shade, then thin down with water. Try 2 parts water to 1 part paint and experiment on a piece of lining paper until you have achieved the desired consistency. Next, make a note of the proportion of paint to water in case you want to make up more of the 'wash' later on. Try out your chosen colour on a small area first. Adjust the proportions of the wash as required.

2 Apply the fresco colour to the wall with a paintbrush, using gentle sweeping movements. The aim is to wash patches of colour thinly over an area, allowing the original plaster to show through. Apply one coat and allow to dry. For a more layered finish, apply one or two more coats.

3 Water down some white emulsion paint in the second bucket until it is very thin and almost translucent (about 8 parts water to 1 part paint). Apply this in the same way and leave to dry.

4 Finally, smooth the wall with fine-grade sandpaper until you have achieved your desired effect. Buff up the wall with a soft cloth to remove dust.

FLOORS

FLOORS

The floor is a defining element in any room. In decorative terms, the floor is background, but when you consider the everyday ways in which we experience space, floors are far from unobtrusive. Barefoot or shod, we walk across floors; we may even sit or lounge on them. For children, the floor is the natural place to play. Floors can amplify or muffle sound; they can supply an insulating warmth in a cold climate or a refreshing coolness in a hot one; they can accommodate spills, knocks and droppages – or they can be less forgiving.

Natural materials work well underfoot. The range of flooring options is so great that almost any practical requirement in the home can be easily met. Pure wool carpeting is warm, soft and gentle on tender young knees; stone, brick or terracotta tiles withstand the daily battering of household traffic in entrance halls; linoleum – surprisingly, a wholly natural product – provides a washable surface for kitchens and bathrooms. Deciding which material is suitable for a particular location means first taking account of its inherent properties, performance and maintenance needs.

If natural flooring fits the bill in practical terms, aesthetically it is miles ahead of its synthetic counterparts. Any change in a synthetic material as a result of use is generally a change for the worse. Natural materials, on the other hand, wear well, which not only means they are durable but also that signs of use contribute depth and character to the surface, a 'patina' that can be both instinctively pleasing and reassuring. Old stone or brick floors last for centuries and look better and better with the passing of years. If properly cared for, wood, too, mellows and ages well. Good quality wool carpet has a not inconsiderable lifespan, equalled by

Rocks and pebbles inlaid in stone offer traditional domestic flooring using indigenous materials. Indestructible, dust-free and gloriously textured, their appeal is truly three dimensional (LEFT).

Painted panelling and timeworn wooden stairs create an enveloping cosiness in a steep stairwell. A stripe painted above the dado (chair) rail punctuates the transition from panelling to plaster (BELOW LEFT).

Totally white walls, ceiling and floors are put into dramatic relief with blue-and-white geometric rugs (RIGHT).

natural fibre coverings such as sisal and jute; with proper maintenance, the initial investment will be repaid by years of service and good looks. Our appreciation of these surfaces has a lot to do with their textural, tactile qualities: the floor, after all, unlike the walls or ceiling, is a surface with which we have direct, physical contact.

As a background to most decorative schemes, natural flooring is inherently complementary. The neutral tones of wood, stone, terracotta and natural

fibres are easy on the eye. But natural materials need not be unassuming. Wood can be stained or painted, wool carpeting dyed in any conceivable shade, and new ranges of sisal and jute coverings include examples in bold patterns and strong, clear colours.

Natural floors work well in combination. There is no need to worry about clashes of style or abrupt changes of mood from room to room or area to area. Brick meets wood, stone meets sisal, and the change of pace is lively

but never jolting. An added advantage is that most natural floors make a good base for rugs, and the layering of kelims, dhurries or rag runners over floorboards, natural fibre, wool or stone just adds to the richness of effect.

Carpeting

Wall-to-wall carpeting is a classic contemporary flooring. For those who are interested in a more traditional version of the natural look, carpet remains a good solution. It provides a seamless, understated background; it is warm, soft, quiet and easy to maintain. Although not as durable as some other natural materials, wool carpeting generally holds up well in most circumstances, kitchens, bathrooms and utility areas excepted.

Wool is the basic ingredient of good-quality carpet; for a wholly natural product choose one hundred per cent wool. The initial investment is much higher than carpeting that includes a substantial proportion of synthetic fibres, but the difference in overall quality is significant. Synthetic fibres, such as nylon and acrylic, increase the lifespan of a carpet and lower its price, so choosing pure wool also involves a slight sacrifice in terms of longevity.

Carpet is available in a wide range of colours and textures. If you stay within the bounds of the neutral range – greys, off-whites, sandy or biscuit tones – a livelier texture than plain cut pile can provide additional character. Specialist firms produce wool carpet in flatweave, bouclé or embossed designs that are exceptionally attractive and luxurious.

The environmental worthiness of a pure wool carpet can be compromised if you fit it over synthetic underlay. Felt, which is composed of a blend of jute and animal hair, is a natural alternative. 'Organic' carpet adhesive is available for sticking down jute-backed carpet, but most high-quality woven carpet should be stretched and nailed to gripper strips by a professional carpet fitter.

Natural fibre floorings

An undoubted success story of recent years has been the rise in popularity of natural fibre floorings such as coir, sisal, jute and rush matting. As with many such 'discoveries', there is nothing new about the use of these materials. Matting has been employed as a serviceable covering for floors ever since medieval times, and is but a small step in sophistication away from the loose rush or straw-strewn floors of ancient castles and manor houses.

Natural fibre matting was originally valued for practical rather than aesthetic reasons (although George IV is said to have chosen it as a sympathetic foil for the Oriental furnishings and decoration at Brighton Pavilion). The shift of application from passageway and doorstep to drawing room, however, has largely been a more recent phenomenon. The contemporary taste for simplicity has led to an appreciation of matting for its own sake, rather than for its ability to shrug off dirt and debris.

There is now available a variety of different fibres, each with its own characteristics and range of applications. The cheapest is seagrass, a smooth, hard fibre grown in paddy-like fields. Seagrass is tough and versatile; it is also anti-static, comfortable and durable. The fibre is virtually impermeable, which makes such coverings exceptionally stain- and dirt-resistant. For the same reason, however, seagrass cannot be dyed; the

Huge Cretan urns stuffed with cochineal-coloured branches make a dramatic statement in this living room. The honey tones of a stripped floor are complemented by a bound sisal rug and autumn colours (LEFT).

Hardwearing and environmentally friendly, seagrass matting is perfect for rooms where its uneven texture and natural colour complements neutral walls and furnishings (FAR LEFT).

New wood-block flooring is both smart and easy to keep clean. Ensure any new wood has been obtained from sustainable sources. The spare elegance of this hallway is enhanced by wooden slatted blinds.

only way of introducing colour to its natural shades of tan and reddish yellow is to weave in coloured weft strings.

Coir, which comes from the coconut husk, makes another robust, affordable floor covering. Traditionally used in doormats, coir is coarse and prickly underfoot, which tends to rule it out in locations such as bedrooms. Coir is available in a variety of weaves, including bouclé, basketweave and herringbone, and in a range of strong colours, from forest green to vibrant red, as well as in neutral tones. In colourful striped or chevron patterns, coir can look very sophisticated and stylish, but the basic variety is an ideal country covering and an excellent base for rugs.

Sisal is derived from *Agave sisalana*, a dark green spiky bush that grows in the subtropics. It comes in a wide variety of weaves from plaid to herringbone, and in a host of colours from indigo to scarlet. Unlike the rather forthright aesthetic of seagrass and coir, the softer texture of sisal offers the elegance of carpet, and can be used in bedrooms where an element of softness underfoot

is required. For even greater comfort and sophistication, there is a new type of natural flooring available in which sisal fibres are blended with wool.

Jute, the softest of all the natural fibre materials, and consequently the least robust, comes from a plant native to India; its fibres have long been imported to make rope and carpet backing. As a floor covering, jute is available bleached or in natural, pastel or strong colours and in a range of weaves.

Rush is the most expensive of all the natural fibre coverings. As medieval matting, made from heavy, plaited strips, it can be made up into any width – to fit a whole room, as a large mat or as a runner. It should not be used on stairs. Rush matting requires regular sprinkling with water to maintain its condition and makes a good flooring for naturally damp areas such as conservatories.

Many natural fibre coverings are susceptible to wear from castors, so additional protection under chair and sofa legs is usually recommended. High, spiky heels can also damage them. Except for medieval matting, most types

of matting are not suitable for really damp or humid locations, which rules out bathrooms, and the coarser weaves may prove hazardous on stairs. Seagrass can be used on stairs if it is laid with the grain parallel to the tread. Most of these coverings are latex-backed and can be fitted over underlay or stuck to the floor. Sisal, coir and jute do stain, and proprietary stain inhibition treatments are available; otherwise maintenance is similar to that for carpeting.

Wood

Wood has been used as flooring for centuries and its long history as a building material underscores its fundamental appeal. Of all natural materials, it is perhaps the most domesticated. Wood, if well-maintained, is long-lasting and improves with the years. It is robust enough to withstand everyday traffic and wear, yet more comfortable and giving than harder materials such as tile and stone. The finest wood floors are among the most attractive of all surfaces, but even worn and battered floorboards can be reclaimed to provide a background which offers character and beauty.

The most economical way of acquiring a good wooden floor is to renovate existing boards. Most older houses have wood floors, particularly on upper levels. In Victorian or Edwardian terraced or semi-detached houses, the floorboards are likely to be made of softwood, usually pine or deal, while purpose-built mansion block flats of the same period may have original parquet, wood block or strip floors in hardwood.

Restoring or improving battered floorboards is largely a matter of effort rather than expense. Depending on the state of the floor, you may need to sink nailheads, block gaps with filler or fillets of wood, nail down loose boards and

replace damaged or rotten ones. If the boards have been concealed beneath carpeting or other types of covering, they may only require thorough cleaning with hot water and strong detergent, together with a little hand sanding to remove any stubborn marks. But most old boards, particularly if they have been left exposed for considerable periods of time, will need to be power-sanded to remove coats of varnish, wax, stain or paint, or simply to deep-clean and level them. This is where the hard work comes in. Even with an electric drum sander, sanding is backbreaking

work. To operate the machine safely, follow the instructions from the rental shop to the letter; you should always wear a protective mask to avoid inhaling dust, and dispose of the sanded dust carefully as it constitutes a fire hazard. Sand first diagonally across the boards, then again in the opposite direction, and finally with the grain. Sand the margins of the floor with an edge sander. Wipe the floor clean of any dust residue after you have finished.

Old hardwood floors in the form of wood strip, block or parquet may be solid or veneered. Either type can be

A timber house with barely a synthetic material or fabric in sight is a tribute to the natural ethos. The easy elegance which flows from the convergence of basic wood, off-white tones and splashes of black to define the space, reflect the simplicity that results from a true sympathy with nature.

The appeal of wooden floorboards is universal and enhances the complete spectrum of room styles from the clean-lined and contemporary to the more rustic. Laid in long, broad planks in a variety of tones – from pale and sun-bleached to mellow honey – and paired with metal and glass furnishings, a wood floor is the ideal foundation for modern living (ABOVE).

The spare, sinuous curves of these weathered stairs have been emphasized with a sympathetic wall colour of faded ochre. Beaten-up floorboards and stairs such as these can be preserved and protected with a regular application of linseed oil or beeswax (RIGHT).

sanded in the same way as boards, but you must check that if the floor is veneered, the veneer is thick enough to withstand the treatment.

Clean or sanded boards should not be left in an unfinished condition as they will quickly degrade, splinter and mark. You can seal, wax, varnish, stain or paint, depending on the effect you wish to create. The orangey tint of stripped pine has fallen out of favour in recent years and can prove a little dominating and harsh. One answer is to lighten the basic tone of the wood by treating it with a bleach solution or lime paste or by rubbing white paint well into the grain prior to the final finish. This will not trick anyone into mistaking pine for a more costly hardwood, but will lighten the wood into a more reticent shade.

Some synthetic floor sealants are extremely toxic and manufacturers recommend wearing protective masks, gloves and clothing during application, as well as keeping rooms well ventilated until the finish dries. It is also advisable not to occupy the room until the vapours have dispersed. Polyurethane is a common base of synthetic sealants, and tends to yellow unattractively with time. Primers and finishes based on natural resins and oils provide equivalent protection, but are non-toxic, and organic alternatives to synthetic wood stains, seals and varnishes are now available. You can tint a sealant with a natural stain or pigment. Liquid beeswax makes a good, water-resistant finish for wooden floors, enhancing the grain and giving off a pleasant smell.

New wooden flooring ranges from the fairly expensive to the very expensive. Ready-made wood floors come in hardwood strip, wood block, parquet or mosaic; alternatively you can lay boards according to your own design and specification. It is best to choose either

locally produced hardwood or woods from sustainably managed plantations. Major retailers are now becoming increasingly responsive to the demands of environmentally aware consumers and will label products clearly, detailing the wood's provenance. Tropical hardwoods, such as teak and mahogany, are among the most endangered varieties. Oak, North American maple, beech, ash, sycamore and lime are all good flooring materials, each with its own characteristics of colour, tone and grain.

Aside from stiletto heels and cigarette burns, which erode the sealant and let water through, wooden floors are able to withstand most ordinary domestic usage. Once a seal or finish has begun to wear, however, it should be renewed.

Cork

Cork tiles make unpretentious, natural floors. Produced by stripping the outer bark of the cork oak, *Quercus suber*, a native of southern Europe, cork is a renewable resource as the tree replaces the bark it has lost, and little waste is generated during its production.

From a practical point of view, cork is hardwearing, is an effective insulator against cold and noise, and provides a cushioning underfoot that is both comfortable and forgiving. Traditional applications include bathrooms and kitchens. Cork can be left unsealed to take advantage of its absorbent qualities, or can be treated with organic primers and waxes to increase water-resistance and durability. Organic adhesives are available for laying.

Linoleum

Where water-resistance is a high priority, in kitchens and bathrooms, for example, linoleum provides a natural alternative to PVC or vinyl floor coverings. Lino has grim associations for those who

remember the utilitarian quality of early designs as well as the material's tendency to crack, but modern linoleum is a vastly improved product, both in performance and appearance.

Lino is made from linseed oil, wood flour, chalk, ground cork and resins, baked and pressed onto jute or hessian backing. Good-quality lino is thick, strong and flexible; it is available in either sheet or tile form, and in a host of colours, patterns and textures. An expanse of glossy off-white lino makes a pristine floor for any light-filled room; for a more decorative effect, use cut-out shapes in different colours or assemble an intricate pattern out of tiles.

Lino is anti-static and resists burns and chemical damage. It will rot if it is laid over a damp floor. Organic adhesive is available for laying, and no seal is necessary.

Bricks and tiles

Floors made of brick, terracotta, quarry tiles, or other materials whose basic ingredient is clay, have an innate visual warmth which belies the hardness of the surface. Instantly suggestive of country settings, these mellow floors, with their subtle earth tones of brownish red, buff and ochre, are extremely long-lasting and homely in appearance. They make good sense in areas that connect outdoors to in, where they offer both a practical and sympathetic transition.

The natural variation in colour and surface from tile to tile or brick to brick is part of the charm of the material. Brick lends itself to different rhythmical arrangements, such as herringbone patterns and basketweave, which enhance its liveliness; old bricks, which can be reclaimed from salvage yards, make exceptionally characterful floors. Quarry tiles or other rustic terracotta varieties acquire a pleasingly pitted

surface with age and wear; like bricks, they don't require sealing or polishing.

On the downside, these materials tend to be physically cold, noisy and unyielding – most breakable objects will shatter if they are dropped on a brick or tile floor. Many of these materials are considerably heavier than other types of flooring, which may rule out their use on upper levels or on unreinforced floors, and installation can often be very disruptive and costly. Brick is also especially porous and will stain.

Stone steps topped with chunky quarry tiles echo the floors above and below the stairwell. Their rich earth tones complement the deep red painted shutters in sharp contrast to the whitewashed walls elsewhere in the house (ABOVE).

Oversized stone tiles create a sense of space in a square entrance way where the bare plaster walls have been deepened slightly with dusk pink to reflect and refract light from the floor. Larger versions of these tiles are used in the adjoining room (TOP RIGHT).

Stone

Natural stone is among the most beautiful of all flooring materials. Its noble aesthetic does come with a hefty price tag, but stone has unique presence, and its sober dignity is equally at home in contemporary and period rooms. Stone is available in a huge range of colours and textures, from the grey-green sheen of slate to the muted granular tones of sandstone to the cold, polished opulence of marble.

Salvage yards dealing in reclaimed materials may be a good source of old stone slabs or marble tiles; if you are choosing new stone, a type quarried locally will be less expensive and more in keeping than imports.

Stone has many of the same basic disadvantages as other types of hard flooring: it is cold, hard, noisy, heavy and difficult to install. Some varieties are more porous than others; sealing may compromise character and alter colour.

Rugs

Rugs can be treated as floor-level accessories or can take on a more positive role. Aside from their decorative impact, rugs soften less comfortable floors. They can be used to enliven an expanse of plain flooring, define seating

An inspired use of tiles as a shower tray creates a roughly textured surface reminiscent of faded Roman frescoes (RIGHT).

Terracotta tiles can be bordered with pebbles to create a chequerboard effect (FAR RIGHT).

Cotton rag runners in muted shades and with a pleasantly irregular weave make the perfect complement to white-painted wooden stairs, tongue-and-groove panelling and simple furnishings in a country cottage.

or eating areas or provide an instant economical transformation. For safety, rugs covering smooth or hard flooring should be laid over non-slip mats.

Homely braided, hooked or cotton rag rugs are among the cheapest of all flooring solutions. They come in all shapes and sizes, from room-size rugs to mats and runners; their simplicity is in keeping with spare contemporary settings as well as cosy country cottages. Only slightly more refined are cotton dhurries from India and other indigenous flatweave rugs such as serapes and kelims. At the top end of the price scale, are hand-knotted Persian or Oriental carpets in silk or wool.

Painted floorcloths (canvas painted with thick pigment) were popular from the early eighteenth century until the advent of linoleum. These often featured geometric designs but more lavish pictorial effects were also produced. The more simple designs can be tried out today.

Natural fibres such as coir, sisal, seagrass, jute and rush also come in mats and runners as well as in room-sized coverings. Some of the more exuberant variations on this basic theme include bold checkered or stencilled coir rugs, soft fringed jute rugs in strong colours, jauntily striped jute runners and sisal rugs with bright contrast edging.

POLKA-DOT STENCILS

Although eggshell (lustre) paint is often used on floors for a tough finish, a water-based white organic paint has been used here for a more distressed look: it wears with age rather than staying a pristine, solid colour. As long as you apply several layers of matt natural varnish, the paint should not chip off easily, but will develop a naturally distressed finish in time. Use organic paint in rooms which don't get heavy foot traffic, such as bedrooms and guest rooms.

If you want to try a more complex design, try varying the size and colour of the polka-dots still further. Or try using chevrons and diamonds, or wavy-line motifs. See page 57 for a stained and striped floor.

MATERIALS

Water-based white organic paint
   (2.5 lits/½ gall covers 25 sq m/82 sq ft)
Water-based lilac and yellow organic paint
10cm (4in) paintbrush
Acetate stencil paper
Craft knife
Pair of compasses
Steel tape measure
Masking tape
Stencil brushes
Matt natural varnish and brush,
   or organic wax

PREPARATION

Scrub the floorboards and strip them, if necessary (see page 57).

METHOD

1 Apply the white paint evenly and leave to dry overnight. Depending on the colour and condition of your existing floorboards, you may need to apply two or more coats.

2 For the polka dots, draw a 2.5cm (1in) circle template on the stencil paper with a pair of compasses. Mark a cross at the centre point of the circle. Cut out the template using a craft knife.

3 Decide on the intervals at which the polka dots will be positioned. Using the template and a tape measure, mark out the position of each dot on the floorboards.

4 Secure the stencil with masking tape and use a stencil brush to apply the coloured paint. Leave to dry overnight.

5 Apply several layers of natural varnish, or buff up to a shine with organic wax, according to the level of protection required and amount of wear the floor is likely to receive. Leave each coat to dry before applying the next.

BLEACHED FLOORBOARDS

An eco-friendly but extremely elegant and sophisticated way of treating stripped and sanded boards is to emulate the off-white distressed effect so typical of traditional eighteenth-century Swedish interiors.

The actual process used to bleach the floorboards involved repeated scrubbing with wet silversand, which called for a lot of elbow grease and decades of ageing before the characteristically informal, uneven finish was achieved.

Luckily, a fair approximation of the effect can be obtained in a fraction of the time by other means. Natural varnishes will need renewing more often than polyurethane varieties.

MATERIALS

Raw linseed oil (approximately 2.5 lits/½ gall covers 25 sq m/82 sq ft)
Small tube of zinc-white pigment or tint
Rags

METHOD

1 Mix a small quantity of zinc white into the oil. Apply the mixture to the boards with a rag, rubbing against the grain to begin with, then along it.

2 Leave to dry for 24 hours, then seal it with a matt natural varnish, or simply apply another layer of lightener when the first treatment wears away.

STAINING IN STRIPES

Enhance the natural grain of wooden boards by staining them in a single colour, or create a 'carpet' by applying stain in repeating patterns, such as diamonds, within a containing border. Bare boards, whatever the treatment, should be in good condition before you start so the time and energy spent in preparation is more than worthwhile.

The striped design shown here uses a combination of fir-green and grey tones, achieved by means of a stain simply applied with a paint brush. Natural varnishes usually include resin or linseed oil (which deeply impregnates wood making it water resistant), larch or copal, which allow the wood to breathe and add extra depth of colour compared with synthetic varnishes.

MATERIALS

String	Craft knife
Tape measure	Paint brush
Masking tape	(10cm/4in)
Metre rule or	Green stain
yardstick	Grey stain
Drawing pins	Natural varnish
Pencil	

PREPARATION

1 If you are applying a design to new floorboards, be sure to 'age' them before staining or varnishing: rough them up with a hammer to distress the surface and make a key for the varnish to adhere to.

2 For old floorboards, make sure that all traces of paint or stain have been removed and, if necessary, sand over the surface with a rented industrial sander. Hammer in any loose nails and fill any gaps between the boards with thin slivers of similar wood.

METHOD

1 To mark out the stripes accurately, start from the centre of the room. You can find the centre point by pinning two pieces of string diagonally from corner to corner and marking the point at which they cross.

2 Mark out your stripes using string and drawing pins. The stripes shown here run across rather than along the boards to create a more unusual effect.

3 Next, mark the edges of the stripes with a pencil and metre rule, and score along each line with a craft knife. This will make a neat edge that will prevent the stains from running into each other.

4 Lay masking tape along each marked-out line, taking care not to cover the groove you have just incised.

5 Apply the stain thinly with a paint brush using gentle sweeping movements. You can dilute it with water to obtain a lighter shade for wider stripes, as here. Leave to dry for 24 hours before applying a natural varnish of your choice. Remember to keep the room in which you are working well ventilated.

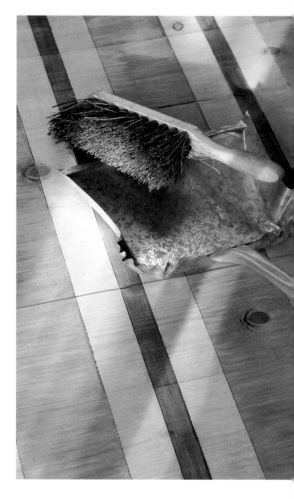

WINDOWS
AND
DOORS

WINDOWS AND DOORS

A wisp of filmy muslin knotted to form the most basic of pelmets (valances) filters the light in an all-white room (ABOVE).

The neat tailoring of a ticking blind (shade) provides a sympathetic accompaniment to Scandinavian-style decor (RIGHT).

Windows are one of the most expressive of all architectural features, defining the character of a room by means of their shape, size, proportion and position. By law, all 'habitable' rooms must have a window, acknowledging the fundamental importance of light and ventilation for health. But, aside from these basic practical needs, windows are also natural focal points; we are almost instinctively drawn to views, light and air. The window opening offers the closest connection to the outside world, and it is a connection we are curiously lost without. There is something profoundly disturbing about a windowless room.

Making the most of windows has little to do with creating swathes of drapery with all the trimmings. Treating the window as a clothes horse tends to ignore two of its main functions – its role as an architectural feature and its affect on light in an interior.

The natural approach to decorating sets out to complement rather than smother the aesthetic and practical features which make windows so appealing. Light is an ally when it comes to revealing the textural beauty of homespun fabric; the innate simplicity of natural window treatments does not compromise what windows have to offer.

Doors and other interior openings may not command the same level of attention as windows, but they do merit a little thought. In many cases, it may just be a matter of enhancing the natural finish of wood with stains, waxes or other treatments. But doors or partitions that are unsympathetic to the style and character of the interior can easily be replaced; and this simple alteration often has a surprising impact.

Letting in the light
A curious aspect of the history of interiors is the changes of attitude towards natural light. In the eighteenth century, people could not have too much of it. Windows were as large and numerous as technology and purse strings would allow, and window coverings tended to be relatively simple compared to the elaborate furnishings elsewhere in the home. A hundred years later, the opposite approach prevailed and great pains were taken to dress windows in layers of fabric, creating the sepulchral gloom so fashionable at the time. But by the end of the nineteenth century, attitudes were shifting again, and light was tentatively welcomed back into the home.

Today we view light as a positive asset. The sunnier the day, the brighter the room, the better our frame of mind; unlike the Victorians, we tend to find darkened rooms depressing rather than mysteriously spiritual. Our positive response stems from a basic association of light with health and well-being; more prosaically, we no longer have to worry about what light is going to reveal. Clean forms of power and heating mean that gloom has lost its usefulness as a way of obscuring grime.

If we simply wished to allow as much light in as possible, the best solution would be to leave windows uncovered. In some cases this is a perfectly good idea. Exceptionally beautiful windows, which display fine detail or an interesting shape, and which do not expose rooms and their occupants to unwelcome scrutiny or ugly views, can be left to speak for themselves.

The reality is that some form of window covering is usually required, at least for part of the day. Unfortunately, few homes are so wonderfully sited that the windows offer glorious vistas of unspoiled countryside. In most cases, views are far more mundane; in some instances they may even be downright

unpleasant. But if the desire to screen an unlovely aspect is a compelling reason to cover a window, the need for privacy provides an even stronger motivation – an exposed window at night-time tends to generate a sense of insecurity.

A window can be left uncovered and still provide a certain degree of privacy if fully transparent glass is exchanged for a more opaque variety. Various forms of 'obscured' glass – which has a textured surface to prevent clear views while still admitting light – are widely available, but many of the cheaper types can be distinctly unattractive. Sandblasted glass, however, provides the requisite degree of screening but is far better looking. It has an attractive watery grey-green translucency that is particularly at home in bathrooms. Glass can be sandblasted to order to create different patterns of clear and frosted glass within the same pane: one simple way of ensuring privacy while at the same time retaining an outlook is to leave a central 'porthole' of clear glass in a frosted surround. Another glazing alternative is to replace clear panes with antique etched or stained-glass versions. This does not necessarily block views in or out completely, but it does alter the colour and quality of light in a pleasing fashion.

Fabric treatments can also be designed to enhance the quality of light. If you choose a fabric or style that diffuses, filters or otherwise modulates light in some way, you can evoke the inherent vitality and variety of daylight that we experience outdoors. Outside, light levels are rarely static and uniform; light is dappled by trees and foliage, shifted by clouds, constantly changing in intensity. The fracturing of light through slatted blinds, its soft diffusion through woven linen or fine muslin imitates these variations and creates appealing light effects of its own.

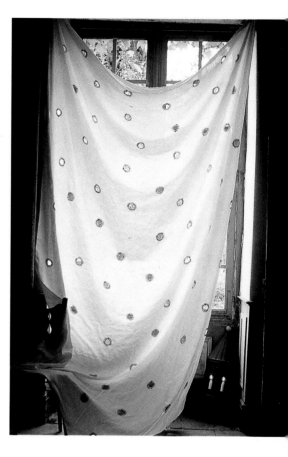

For simple drapery with a twist, customize plain fabric with sewn-on shells, glass beads or cut-out shapes. Small seashells sewn onto a swathe of fine muslin are silhouetted in the light (LEFT).

Holes punched into cotton sheeting add a touch of wit and surprise to an impromptu treatment for French windows (ABOVE).

Light reveals the homespun texture of natural linen hanging at the window (TOP) and enhances the delicacy of intricate drawn thread work enriching a swathe of fine cotton voile (ABOVE).

Cheerful checked curtains in unlined cotton gingham add freshness and vitality to a bathroom (RIGHT).

Types of fabric

Natural fabrics offer a wide range of textures, weights and finishes, from the soft density of linen to the virtual transparency of butter muslin. Cottons and linens have been furnishing mainstays for centuries and provide immense scope in themselves; recently, other fabrics incorporating fibres such as hemp and raffia have extended the natural range even further.

As in other areas, the term 'natural' can be misleading. By checking the label, it is easy enough to determine that a fabric does not include a percentage of synthetic fibres, but exclusion of artificial fibres may not necessarily result in a wholly natural product. Crops such as cotton may be sprayed with pesticides; the fibres can be chlorine-bleached before chemical dyeing; finishes or dressings may be added to promote flame-retardation and other attributes. Unbleached fabric, or fabric that has been coloured with natural dyes, at least guarantees the minimum interference with the basic fibre and the least damage to the environment.

Linen, traditionally used around the home for bed and table linen, has grown in popularity as a furnishing fabric. Like cotton, it is derived from a renewable crop, in this case flax; but unlike cotton, flax is farmed without extensive use of pesticides. Producing linen fibre causes little pollution or waste.

Linen has many other virtues, not least of which is its strength, which actually increases when the fibres are wet. Linen washes and wears extremely well and is exceptionally long-lasting. It is cool to the touch and absorbs humidity, which is why it has always been welcomed next to the skin. Available in a range of weaves from a coarse slub to a fine, silky matt, it is crisp and supremely

Jute tassels can be knotted over a wrought-iron rod (TOP) *or string, rope and raffia lashed to a driftwood pole* (ABOVE).

Sill-length cobalt blue curtains tied back with twine echo the nautical mood of a snug sitting room lined in tongue-and-groove boarding (RIGHT).

textural and makes an excellent furnishing fabric. Unbleached linen is a beautiful taupe colour, but more earthy shades also show off its essential character to advantage. Linen can be used unlined to make soft blinds or simple, elegant curtains that filter rather than completely exclude the light; alternatively, it can be lined for a more robust, light-screening effect.

Cotton is the most versatile of all furnishing materials. Its soft, strong, hard-wearing fibre is the basic ingredient of a whole family of unpretentious fabrics from calico to voile, ticking to duck, many of which are inexpensive, so you can afford to be generous in terms of quantity. Muslin has been used for centuries as a way of diffusing the effect of light; a swathe of muslin thrown over a pole must rate as one of the cheapest and easiest of all window coverings. The stiffer cottons that block light more effectively, such as mattress ticking or duck (available in widths of up to 10ft/3m), are equally affordable and hang very well.

One of cotton's greatest advantages is its receptiveness to dye. Furnishing departments stock cotton in every colour, but for sheer intensity and richness, nothing betters the saturated shades produced by natural dyes. Indigo, madder, turmeric and other vegetable pigments produce colours ranging from subtle to searing.

Silk is the most luxurious of the natural fibres and generates a look of elegance and sophistication. Made from silkworm cocoons, silk is available in a variety of weights and textures, from feather-light chiffons to slubbed shantung. Shantung makes a sumptuous, although expensive, window treatment.

Hessian (burlap), at the opposite end of the spectrum, is a coarse, open-weave fabric made from jute or a blend of jute and hemp. Although its most popular use in the interior has generally been as a serviceable wall covering, hessian can also make simple, rugged-looking blinds (shades) and curtains.

For less conventional, and even instant, window treatments, you can investigate the potential of materials not generally associated with furnishing. Madras cotton bedspreads, lightweight quilted covers, printed cotton or silk saris, sailcloth, artist's canvas and dress fabrics can all take on a new dimension hanging at the window.

Types of treatment

Fabric curtains or blinds are the instinctive choices for most window treatments for a variety of reasons. Convention comes into it, but fabric has more positive advantages, both aesthetic and practical. Relatively lightweight and easy to manipulate, it can be made to hang in soft folds which complement and frame the window opening. Fabric usually offers at least some degree of translucency, unless it is heavily lined, and it is easily cleaned and renewed.

Curtains are traditionally fashioned using heading tape, which draws up the material into a series of gathers or pleats; these provide a foundation for the hooks and rings that suspend the curtains from a track or pole. Heading styles range from simple loose gathering to formal pinched pleats. If you opt for one of these conventional approaches, ensure that the fabric weight is suitable for the heading style. Lighter material generally looks better in loose gathers; fabric with greater body and weight is required for a more tailored, pleated style.

When you are using natural fabrics and colourings, the simplest treatments often work the best. It is not necessary to go to great lengths to obscure curtain headings or means of fixing; a

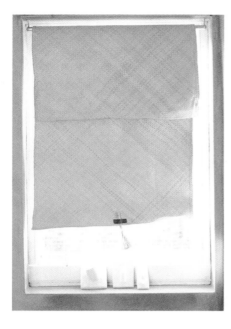

straightforward, unstructured effect suits both material and context.

Less formally, curtains can simply be tied, looped, shirred, clipped or laced onto a pole or rod, making a feature of the way they are hung. Narrow fabric tapes or ribbons sewn along the top of the curtains can be tied directly onto the pole; fabric loops that slide along the pole are another version of the same idea. Ready-made curtains in natural fabrics such as cotton twill or ticking are generally sold in this format. Lighter materials can be given a cased heading and shirred along a rod. Clipping fabric onto a pole or rod using café clips is a virtually instant solution that entails no sewing at all, which makes it ideal for fabrics such as saris or embroidery which you may not want to cut.

Curtains or window coverings made of stiffer material, such as canvas or duck, can be rigged up like sails, lashing the material to a pole or rod with laces threaded through eyelets. Chandlers and yachting supply stores stock a wide range of ropes, pulleys and cleats that can be pressed into service to suggest a nautical look.

Wooden poles can be painted, varnished, waxed or stained; metal rods

are available in a range of styles, from curlicues of wrought iron to polished brass. Thinking laterally, you can also use a host of other items, such as lengths of bamboo, scaffolding tubes, steel ropes and even weathered driftwood, provided whatever you choose can take the weight of the material.

Natural fabrics also lend themselves to informal drapery where a length of material is simply flung over a pole and arranged in loose folds. This type of treatment suits light, fairly translucent fabric such as muslin – be generous with the amount you use and always be prepared to experiment.

Blinds come into their own in situations where full-length curtains would create an obstruction or even a potential hazard, such as in the kitchen. One of the most effective of all fabric blinds is the type that rolls up like an awning and is secured with long fabric ties. Natural unbleached linen works well in this style; for a jauntier look, try striped ticking. Alternatively, Roman or even roller blinds can look good in natural unbleached fabric.

Blinds (shades) can be improvized from a variety of natural materials and ingredients. A length of woven matting makes an instant blind slung over a fine metal rod and trimmed with a small raffia tassel (FAR LEFT).

Fabric is not always the best solution for window treatments. This solid panelled shutter emphasizes the architectural quality of the tiny recessed cottage window (LEFT).

A roll-up fabric blind (shade) makes an elegant counterpoint to a panelled interior. The contrast lining lends graphic definition to a simple treatment. (RIGHT).

cheaper still. For a more substantial cover-up you can fit or renovate folding wooden shutters in the form of either solid or louvred panels.

Finishing touches

Natural decorating is generally identified with a pared-down aesthetic, of which character and visual interest are expressed in the quality of basic materials. But this does not mean you have to rule out trimmings or details. If a window treatment consists of fairly plain curtains in a subdued natural shade, finishing touches such as fringing, tie-backs and tassels can help to provide a little extra definition.

Trimmings are now available in a wide variety of natural materials. Raffia tassels and tie-backs; fringing made of raffia, jute, linen or even horsehair; plaited paper tie-backs and twists of straw won't compromise the basic approach, but will supply additional textural interest. Seashells or starfish can take the place of finials, or you can sew tiny shells randomly across the fabric or as a border along the edge.

Doors

Entrances are places of special significance. Doors, which usher you across the threshold, from outdoors to in, from hallway to interior, deserve more than passing consideration. The character, construction and finish of a door provides an eloquent summary of the room it announces, which is why shoddy doors and door furniture are such a let down.

Cheap, modern hollow-core doors are just begging to be replaced. A door should suggest security and structural integrity; if yours do not, no amount of finishing or decoration will make any difference. Old panelled wooden doors are readily available from architectural

Interior doors can help to bring out the architectural character of a space. In this bedroom, a Moorish-style effect is achieved by screening the contents of a built-in wardrobe with pierced wooden panels (ABOVE).

Exterior shutters in simple planking are enlivened by bold arrowhead cutouts in a rugged interpretation of American primitive style (RIGHT).

Ready-made blinds are also available in a range of other materials which accord with the natural look. For flexible light control, slatted wooden Venetian blinds are a good solution and come in a range of colours. Light slanting in through half-open slats creates moody atmospheric effects. Blinds made of woven grasses or split cane have a tropical look and are eminently affordable. Pleated paper blinds are

salvage yards and it should not be difficult to match style and period if your home has been subject to unsympathetic conversion. New wooden doors are also manufactured in traditional styles. Stable or cottage-style doors in planking have a rough-and-ready simplicity that suits rustic surroundings.

Glazed door panels let in light and create a greater sense of openness. Door glazing can also arouse a feeling of expectation and add a certain richness to entrances. Small panes of stained or etched glass are a beautiful feature of many Victorian and Edwardian doors; in the designs of Charles Rennie Mackintosh doors were often enhanced by small panels of leaded glass depicting abstract natural motifs, or simple squares of jewel-like colour arranged in a small grid.

The most common way of renovating old doors is to strip away layers of paint and varnish and leave the wood exposed. If you adopt this approach, there is no need to varnish or seal with synthetic products; beeswax or linseed oil rubbed well into the grain will nourish and protect the wood. Like other interior joinery, doors are usually made of a softwood such as pine, traditionally considered unworthy of exposure. If you do not wish to leave the wood bare, however, there are a number of finishes that will retain its 'woody' character while softening the effect of raw pine. One of these is to apply liming paste, which knocks back the orangey tone of the wood and gives it a gently distressed appearance. Wood stains and tinted wood varnishes (which are available in environmentally friendly form) alter the basic colour but do not obscure the grain. Special paint techniques such as graining, combing or crackleglazing will supply textural interest and a more overtly faked finish.

Door furniture is the detail within the detail. The designers of the Arts and Crafts Movement used broad iron strap hinges and hand-wrought latches as a means of expressing constructional honesty. These features tend to work most effectively on solid oak or cottage-style planked doors; in other cases, it may be a question of searching out appropriate period doorknobs and latches from salvage yards, or you may

The discreet charm of etched glass echoes the refinement of architectural detail in this cool entranceway. Glazed doors bring light into the heart of the interior (LEFT).

The basic appeal of a stripped and waxed pine door adds a homely dimension to a contemporary living area (ABOVE).

prefer the traditional understatement of plain white china.

There are situations where a door may not be the best solution for an entranceway. If you do not want the interruption of space, light and view that a door entails, you can simply remove it altogether. You may also wish to remove the wooden architrave that provides evidence of the door's former existence; the raw edges of the opening can be plastered in with the wall and decorated to match, or picked out with a colour. But an entrance without a door is still an entrance, and you may wish to signal its importance by retaining the architrave or by adding a decorative border, such as stones pressed into wet plaster or a stencilled edging.

In traditional Japanese houses, doorways were often hung with swinging bamboo bead curtains or a short banner-like cloth cut into strips that allowed the free passage of air and traffic. The advantage of such treatments is that they

diffuse the force of the wind, while permitting light and air to flow through. You can make your own bead curtain if you fancy a laborious task, or install a Japanese-style version in bamboo and wooden beads; alternatively, a doorway can, of course, be curtained in any of the ways suitable for windows. When curtaining a doorway, ease of operation is an important consideration. Fabric can be suspended from wooden or metal rings that slide freely along a pole or rod. For lightweight material, a simple cased heading may be adequate. Fabric ties, loops or an eyeletted heading are other good alternatives. In a contemporary setting, you could adapt another Japanese idea and fit an opening with a full-height sliding wooden screen panelled in glass or paper.

Both sides of a door need not be painted or finished in the same way. A deep azure blue on the inner surface of this panelled door makes a banner of colour at the entrance to the kitchen (ABOVE).

The distressed finish of this back door, with patches of paint still clinging to the grain, harmonizes with the kitchen cupboards (LEFT).

The solidity of this panelled door has been emphasized by picking out panels in blue. A glass pane has been substituted for one of the panels, providing a tantalizing view from hall to interior (RIGHT).

A fitted wardrobe with a difference: hanging space is cleverly screened behind overlapping cane blinds, framed by the contours of a plywood surround (RIGHT).

The boarded construction of an entrance door is highlighted by bands of soft, natural colour, picking up on the detail of the beamed hall ceiling. A treatment which would have been too emphatic if executed in stronger tones here provides a subtle sense of rhythm that helps to offset the scale of the opening (ABOVE).

AWNING BLIND

This simple blind (shade) can be adapted to suit any room. Use soft butter muslin or calico for a bedroom, cotton gingham or tea-towel linen in a kitchen, or deckchair fabric in a bright living room or children's room. The blind is so easy to make and so economical with fabric that you could ring the changes from winter to summer. A strong, plain treatment is suitable for both lined and unlined curtains.

MATERIALS
Awning canvas
Eyelet pack and hammer
Jute string (thick and thin)
Sewing thread
Pen
Thick upholstery needle or glue
2 U-shaped brackets
    (or 3, if the window is very wide)
Wooden pole 3.75cm
    (1½in) diameter
2 cleats and screws

PREPARATION
Measure the width of your window and cut a piece of fabric to fit, allowing a 5cm (2in) seam allowance on all sides.

METHOD
1 Place fabric right side down and turn in raw edges along both sides. Machine-sew a 1.25cm (½in) hem down each side. To strengthen, also sew along outer edges of hem. Turn in raw edges at top and bottom of fabric and machine-sew a 5cm (2in) hem at either end.

2 Measure 2.5cm (1in) in from either edge at the top of the blind and mark the position of the first eyelets with a pen. Divide up the remaining width of fabric into regular intervals, leaving approximately 12.5cm (5in) space between each one. Use your eyelet pack as per instructions to insert the eyelets along the top of the blind. Hammer them in position.

3 Next, unravel enough string to loop through the eyelets in a zigzag fashion and to wind around the pole at each side of the blind and attach to wall cleats (about 3m/10ft). Mark the position of the pole brackets and wall cleats with a pen. Remove the blind from the pole and fix pole brackets, pole and wall cleats in place.

Fold the blind in half horizontally, right sides together, and mark the positions of the jute tassels along the bottom edge of the blind, using the eyelet holes as a guide. To make the jute tassels, bind together approximately 16 lengths of thin jute string, each 20cm (8in) long, using a longer piece of the same string. Knot it in place.

Stick the tassels onto the blind with glue, or, better still, sew them in place using a short piece of string and a thick upholstery needle.

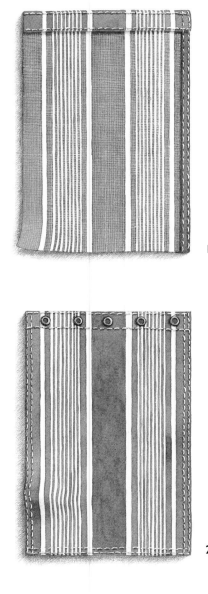

1

2

4 If you want to draw up the blind during the day, fold or roll up the blind to the height you want, then loop two lengths of string over the pole and tie in position at either side of the blind. Or, use two extra lengths of string to suspend the blind.

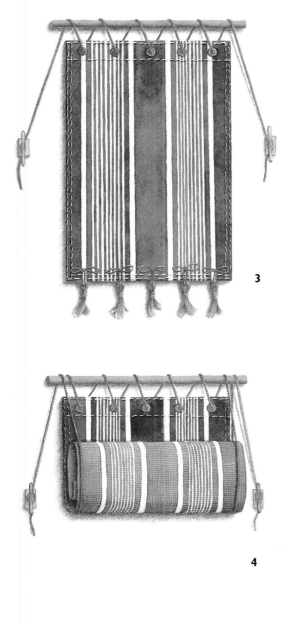

3

4

CURTAINS WITH TIED HEADINGS

These simple informal curtains do away with the need for complicated curtain headings and tracks. Suspended from metal, wooden or chrome poles by loops which are integral to the curtain, any ugly window can be dressed in a matter of hours. The neutral colours and natural textures of calico, pre-shrunk hessian, scrim, ticking or cotton gingham are well suited to this treatment. Alternatively, muslin held with ribbon bows creates a graceful, diaphanous effect.

For a variation on the now-classic metal pole, try using wooden dowelling or even a knarled windfall branch instead. The curtains themselves can be embellished with bows in a contrasting colour or with bound edges in a bold colour to provide added definition. The ties can range from narrow ribbons to fat bows, according to the effect you wish to create. Vary their dimensions to suit the window shape and the room's proportions. To avoid droops forming between the ties, use well-stiffened headings and be sure to place the ties at frequent intervals along the curtain.

MATERIALS
Medium-weight calico or woven cotton
Lining
Metal or wooden pole and 2 support
    brackets (more if the pole is longer
    than 180cm/6ft or if the curtains are
    made from heavy fabric)
Bias binding, calico or buckram
Sewing thread
Pencil

MEASURING UP
Calculate the length of pole by measuring the full curtain extent plus 10–15cm (4–6in) for the finials. Each curtain needs to be 1⅓ times the width of the pole: for example, for a 180cm (6ft) pole you will need two curtains, each 270cm (9ft) wide. Calculate the length of fabric loop you will need by fixing (or holding) the pole in place and measuring where the bottom of each loop should fall. There should be little or no daylight between the curtain and the window frame itself.

METHOD
1 Lay the fabric right-side down. Turn in the raw edges on each side to make a 2.5cm (1in) seam, pin and machine-sew. Along the bottom, turn in the raw edge and machine-sew a 7.5cm (3in) hem.

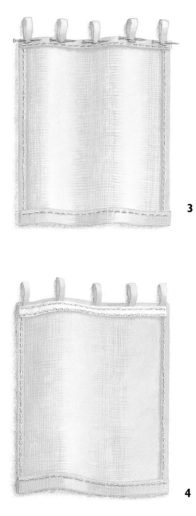

3

4

2 Each loop should be roughly 20cm (8in) apart and 2.5–3.25cm (1–1½in) wide, depending on the length of your pole. Mark with a pencil the position of each end loop; then divide the remaining length into equal segments, marking the position of each loop on the fabric with a pencil.

3 Make up the loops by measuring out your required length and width plus a 12mm (½in) seam allowance all round. Place the fabric right-side down and form a tube by turning in the raw edges

so that they overlap down the centre. Pin, then machine sew in place stitching through both layers of fabric. Turn right side out. Repeat for the other loops.

4 Place the curtain right-side down and position one end of each loop. Bring the other end of each loop over to form an arc and pin in place about 12mm (½in) down from the top edge of the curtain. Take a strip of bias binding or calico the width of the curtain plus, for calico, a 6mm (¼in) seam allowance all round (for bias binding, leave this seam

allowance on at the ends; for buckram, do not include seam allowance).

Turn in the raw edges and pin in place, catching the loops between the binding and the curtain fabric at a depth of 12mm (½in). Machine-sew the binding to the curtain top and bottom, thereby fixing the loops in place.

To make the fabric ties, take a length of fabric measuring approximately 750 x 12mm (30 x ½in). Add a 6mm (¼in) seam allowance. Machine-sew raw edges together (right sides facing), then turn right side out.

DECORATIVE DOOR TREATMENTS

The patina and warmth of stripped and treated wooden doors is generally easy on the eye and offers a subtle introduction to any room. Doors treated in this way can work well in combination with either neutral or rich colours and can form a key feature of a wall decoration scheme. The following wood treatments allow you to both protect and enhance the natural wood of floors, panelling and skirting boards as well as doors. Natural stains will enable you to alter the colour of new, raw pine or stripped old wood, either by darkening the wood's natural tones or by changing the colour completely. (For suppliers of natural stains and colour washes, see Sources list.)

NATURAL BEESWAX

Many old doors, once stripped of several layers of paint and sanded down to accentuate the grain, need only a generous application of natural beeswax to feed and protect them. Beeswax can be used on sealed or unsealed wood and provides a water-resistant finish. It can also be used on stripped wood floors.

MATERIALS

Fine-grade sandpaper
2 soft cloths, one for applying polish, one for buffing up
Organic wood filler (0.4 lits/¾pt covers 4 sq m/13 sq ft)
Natural beeswax polish (0.4 lits/¾pt covers 20 sq m/65½ sq ft)

PREPARATION

An old door should be stripped of all its paint, either by having it professionally dipped or by steaming off the paint and giving it a thorough sanding down, using rough-grade sandpaper. Fill any big cracks or gaps with organic wood filler, but generally leave any small-scale surface imperfections alone.

METHOD

1 Once the door is stripped of paint, sand it down with fine sandpaper.

2 Use a soft cloth to apply beeswax to the whole door. This process calls for vigorous polishing: the more wax you apply and the more effort you put into it, the richer the finished result. Leave the door for several hours to allow the wax to penetrate the wood.

3 Buff up a small area of the door with a soft, clean coth. Check it to ensure you have applied enough beeswax to accentuate the natural grain of the wood and create a clear, honeyed tone. Then buff up the door with the same cloth.

Leave naturally-occuring blemishes such as cracked, uneven edges or double keyholes, alone (ABOVE). They add character to an old door especially once it has been waxed and vigorously polished.

CRACKLEGLAZE ANTIQUE FINISH

Crackleglaze is a good medium for ageing a brand new door. It is easily applied and, when sealed, provides a permanent finish which has the air of faded antiquity. The crackleglaze itself should always be applied between two layers of water-based emulsion. This sandwich of paint-glaze-paint allows the surface of the glaze to crack and split, creating a peeled patina reminiscent of ageing paint. When all three layers have been applied, the door should be sealed with a natural varnish such as shellac.

MATERIALS

5cm (2in) paintbrush
Ochre water-based emulsion (latex)
    (2.5 lits covers 25 sq m/82 sq ft)
Fine-grade sandpaper
Soft cloth for buffing
Commercially prepared crackleglaze
    paint (500ml covers 6 sq m/20 sq ft)
White water-based emulsion (latex)
    (2.5 lits covers 25 sq m/82 sq ft)
Natural varnish such as shellac
    (0.75 lits covers 7.5 sq m/25 sq ft)

METHOD

1 On a new door, paint on a thin coat of yellow ochre emulsion and leave to dry.

2 Sand back the paint to make the colour 'fade' slightly, then buff up the surface with a soft cloth. Next, apply a thin coat of crackleglaze all over the door and leave to dry.

3 Finish off with a thin coat of white emulsion, watered-down in the proportion of 2 parts water to 1 part paint. Allow to dry, then gently sand back to allow the glaze and yellow ochre to show through.

4 Seal the door with a natural shellac varnish to protect the glaze.

LIMED WOOD

Traditionally, liming was a treatment applied to stripped oak in which a white paste filler was used to fill the grain of the wood and create a smooth surface that could be sanded to accentuate the grain and stain it a white-grey colour. (See bleaching floorboards, page 56, for an alternative method of creating a limed effect.)

Nowadays there are a number of liming treatments available which look authentic and are really quick and simple to apply to any kind of wood. The door shown (right) is a new one, but you can easily apply liming wax to an old door provided that it is completely stripped of any paint or varnish and then sanded down.

MATERIALS

Steel wool
Liming wax (500ml covers 6 sq m/
    20 sq ft)
Soft cloth for buffing
Natural varnish such as shellac
    (optional; 0.75 lits covers 7.5 sq m/
    25 sq ft)

METHOD

1 Scour the new or stripped door with steel wool to accentuate the grain.

2 Rub on the liming wax with a soft cloth, working against the grain of the wood. Repeat the process, working along the grain. Check that the liming wax has filled all the open textural markings in the wood.

3 Leave the wax for an hour or so to harden, then buff it up with a soft cloth. After 24 hours the door can be given a coat of natural varnish, such as shellac, to protect the surface. Alternatively, apply a natural beeswax to the door and then rub with a soft rag.

FITTINGS
AND
FURNISHINGS

FITTINGS AND FURNISHINGS

Draped muslin provides a serene canopy above a comfortable daybed and echoes the informal branches of a bougainvillea on a Mediterranean arched terrace (ABOVE).

The simple elegance of wood and whitewash is a timeless solution for this tiny seaside home, where mismatching pieces of furniture work well against a backdrop of single-colour walls and floors (RIGHT).

Natural decorating is concerned just as much with the contents of a room as it is with background and finish. Furnishing is where the fun begins. Against the neutrality of pale plastered walls or natural fibre flooring, you can add layers of colour and interest to make the room come alive.

The sparseness and lack of density implied in natural decorating does not necessarily entail a minimalist approach to furnishing. Comfort is essential, and no successful room can ever be created without taking account of the physical needs of its occupants.

In recent years, interiors have become increasingly 'unfitted', and traditional forms of free-standing storage have been reintroduced and reinterpreted. This approach provides scope for eclecticism and originality, where furniture from different sources and periods blend happily together to create a spontaneous

and personal look. One or two well-made modern pieces – a beautiful table, a sofa, or a good bed, for example – can serve as the foundation for room arrangement, with heirlooms, junk shop finds and a few good basics added to the mix. You won't necessarily be able to create the effect overnight, but the result will have the natural unforced quality that comes when rooms are allowed to evolve over time.

Types of furniture

Furniture made of natural materials has an obvious pedigree. Although we may well turn a blind eye to the synthetic ingredients of wall finishes and flooring, we tend to be far more discriminating when it comes to choosing chairs and tables. However, what you see isn't necessarily what you get. Some types of furniture, particularly upholstered pieces, often incorporate a significant

proportion of synthetic material: fillings made of foam or artificial fibre can be concealed beneath environmentally friendly calico. Varnishes and other finishes provide other means for synthetic elements to infiltrate otherwise natural products. Nevertheless, modern retailers are increasingly addressing the ecological concerns of their customers and there has been a real attempt in recent years to use only species of wood in furniture production that come from sustainably managed sources. In many cases, furniture is labelled to that effect.

Another way of guaranteeing a natural product is to patronize the work of young furniture designers who are exploring the use of natural materials in a contemporary fashion. Cabinetmakers and craftspeople working in wood inevitably have an acute awareness of material and its provenance. (British woodworkers, for example, are still exploiting the windfall offered by the damage caused by the hurricane of 1989.) Commissioning pieces from such sources is not necessarily expensive. Involvement in the craft process, perhaps even to the extent of specifying materials, can enormously increase one's appreciation of a furnished piece, as well as offering the satisfaction of helping to support the work of individual artisans. Handcrafted goods revive the connection between maker and material, which has long been overshadowed by industrial production.

The choice is broader for those content with items which are simply as natural as possible, rather than scrupulously environmentally friendly. You can create a natural 'look' with a wide range of good-looking contemporary furniture in wood, cane, wicker and metalwork, from scrubbed oak refectory tables and rattan sofas to rush-bottomed kitchen chairs. In many

designs, the warmth and tactility of natural materials provides a perfect complement to clean, modern lines – the look is simple, but not stark. Many such pieces work well in combination, which makes it easy to avoid the deadening effect of the coordinated suite. Canvas director's chairs pulled up to wooden dining tables, rattan side tables with metal legs accompanying deep squashy sofas covered in linen, dressers flanked by slatted garden chairs all help to create the sort of unselfconscious, informal arrangements that evoke the natural look.

A muslin canopy increases the sense of enclosure in this recessed platform bed which maximizes space and provides an additional storage area in a small room (LEFT).

Furniture that is made from reclaimed timber can be elegant as well as kind to the environment (ABOVE).

furniture, made of paper-wrapped wire woven together over a bentwood frame, has become a contemporary classic. Simple, French-style folding park chairs are equally versatile basics.

Reclaiming and revamping old furniture is another sound natural option. Salvage yards, junk shops and antique markets are all good sources of interesting and original pieces that may have many years of life ahead of them. Old pine kitchen tables, bentwood chairs, simple stools, oak settles, country dressers and chests of drawers, Windsor and ladderback chairs all display a forthright simplicity that goes well with the natural look. You can re-finish such pieces by stripping away previous coats of paint or varnish and oiling or waxing the wood. Alternatively, you can apply washes of water-based paint for a matt, distressed effect: white tinted with ochre and washed over pine produces a faded, chalky finish; sea-greens, blues and soft reds have a cheerful folk-art appeal.

Furniture and fittings produced for commercial or institutional purposes can be equally useful in a domestic situation. Glass-fronted shop fittings and display shelves provide commodious storage for bedding and clothes. School cupboards and lockers can house books, crockery and linen. Steam trunks and wicker laundry hampers make flexible catch-alls for toys, shoes or blankets. Shelving, the most basic form of storage, is generally constructed from synthetic boards such as MDF (medium-density fibreboard) or particleboard, which are extremely strong and dimensionally stable. These materials, however, may be potentially harmful as the resins which bind the fibres contain formaldehyde. For a more natural approach, you can make use of reclaimed timber, such as old floorboards or scaffolding planks. Basic boards can be painted or stained

Wicker, wood and cotton produce a happy combination of textures and colours in natural-based interiors. Campaign furniture, designed for travel, and Lloyd Loom chairs, intended for outdoor use, come into their own, their simple shapes complemented by natural fabrics (ABOVE AND RIGHT).

Nowadays garden furniture is more likely to be found indoors than out. Wickerwork or twiggy, Appalachian-style chairs and tables, steamer chairs, metal café tables and other pieces originally designed for the conservatory or *al fresco* life on the verandah, bring their association with natural settings into the living room. Lloyd Loom garden

to tone with the wall, or for a more rugged effect, washed with a thin coat of plaster or gesso.

Standing screens provide a flexible means of partitioning space. Basic frameworks made from hardwood, softwood, bamboo or metal can be covered with a variety of materials, including woven rattan panels, thick paper and plain calico. Screens made of hinged wooden panels, stained, painted or waxed, are simple enough to construct yourself.

Perhaps the single most important piece of furniture in our homes is the bed. Money spent on a good-quality mattress and base is never wasted, yet some of the simplest beds are also the healthiest and most natural. A Japanese-style futon on a low wooden or metal platform is thoroughly ecological; alternatively, opt for sprung mattresses made from natural fibres. Slatted timber bases or metal bedsteads allow air to circulate freely. Choose feather- rather than foam-filled pillows.

Hanging space for clothes can be rigged up very simply by fitting an alcove with a length of pole or a metal rod and screening the space with curtaining, bamboo, Roman or roller blinds (shades), sliding doors or louvres. Shop rails offer another solution; canvas tent-style 'wardrobes' provide the added advantage of protecting clothes from dust and sunlight.

Kitchens and bathrooms
The kitchen may be the heart of the home, but it can often be the least natural of places. Fitted modern units sealed under laminate worktops have a chilling sterility that is at odds with the basic nurturing function of the room. Even worse, such components can be positively harmful. Particleboard, commonly used in fitted units, may

In a narrow space with small shuttered windows, white walls and fabric enhances its size. Sheer drapes provide an understated screen between a daybed and the rest of the room (LEFT).

Limed wood works well in a room where you want to keep a light look. Commercially prepared liming paste is one method of treating old or new wood once stripped. Alternatively, use water-based white emulsion (latex) and sand down between coats (ABOVE).

well leach formaldehyde and other potentially toxic chemicals may seep out of synthetic paints and finishes used as sealants and waterproofing agents. It is inconsistent if not counter-productive to ensure the food we eat is as organically produced and free of additives as possible, but then proceed to store, cook and prepare it in surroundings that have a polluting effect.

Traditional unfitted kitchens in farmhouses and cottages provide a good role model for the natural kitchen. Food preparation can take place as readily on butcher's blocks and refectory tables as on built-in worktops and free-standing dressers, cabinets and chests offer flexible storage space. The traditional larder, a cool room sited on the external walls of a house and fitted with slate shelves and stone flooring, provides natural refrigeration and excellent

storage conditions for a wide range of foodstuffs. Manufacturers have taken the lead from those reclaiming original pieces of free-standing kitchen furniture and many now produce contemporary unfitted ranges of their own. This can be an expensive option, but the fact that you can take your kitchen with you when you move provides a mitigating factor.

If you prefer at least part of your kitchen to be built in, you can choose solid wood units or have fittings custom-made. This does not have to be as costly as it sounds: a softwood carcase of shelves, cupboards and worktop can be finished with relatively cheap tongue-and-groove door fronts, or even curtaining. For a sleeker effect, you can transform undistinguished units with zinc sheeting, secured with upholstery nails. Worktops made of wood, ceramic or terracotta tiles, granite, marble, steel

Simple garden trellising painted a vivid blue serves as a kitchen unit in a small kitchen whose junk-shop table is disguised with white paint and enhanced by metal café chairs and rope cushions (LEFT).

The clean lines of stainless steel units and fittings in a compact kitchen have been roughed up by the addition of whitewashed wall cladding made from old floorboards (ABOVE).

with the stew. What you probably don't need are gadgets that promise to be labour-saving, but end up consuming space and energy. For a fraction of the cost, good quality pots and pans and a set of high quality knives will serve most requirements equally well.

The kitchen is a power centre that inevitably generates waste. In some countries, notably Germany, waste recycling is mandatory; elsewhere in the world it is largely left to individual conscience. Taking the trouble to fit out separate receptacles for organic, glass, paper and metal waste will provide added incentive for trips to the compost heap or bottle bank.

Unlike the cheery communality of the family kitchen, the bathroom tends to be a private place, where the stresses of the day can be soaked away in peace and quiet. From an ecological point of view, showers are less wasteful of water than baths, and the Japanese practice of washing away dirt under a shower before a relaxing communal soak in a hot tub marries personal hygiene with conservation. Japanese-style soaking tubs tend to be deeper and narrower than Western baths, which helps to retain water heat. Sharing a hot tub with family or friends is an Eastern convention that may never find widespread acceptance in the inhibited West, but the basic principle of separating washing from relaxation is a sound one.

Absorbent finishes and surfaces, such as untreated cork flooring tiles and water-based microporous paints, work well in bathrooms since they allow surfaces to breathe. Wicker and cane furniture suit the humid bathroom climate as much as the conservatory environment for which it was first designed. Ceramic non-slip tiles provide a high degree of water-repellence. Open metal and glass shelving can be used to

The synchronicity of ceramic and terracotta tiles, wood and whitewash work well in bathrooms where surfaces should be smooth and easy to clean. Tiles provide wipeable wall coverings and splashbacks, whereas wood provides a natural warmth on doors and in the form of cladding and shelving (ABOVE AND RIGHT).

or zinc have their own intrinsic beauty and are just as practical as synthetic versions. Inset marble slabs are useful for pastry-making; small pieces of marble can often be bought from salvage yards or stonemasons.

Other traditional kitchen ideas that are worthy of rediscovery include wickerwork drawers for vegetables that need aerating and the redoubtable string shopping bag as an alternative to plastic carriers from the supermarket. Conversely, it is a mistake to hang on to elderly appliances. Modern ovens, for example, are more energy-efficient than older models. One of the best investments of all is the Aga (range); with care and a little expertise, it will last a lifetime and warm the kitchen along

store towels and accessories; if you like the unfitted look, sinks can be housed in freestanding metal 'tables'.

Covers and accessories

Cushions, throws, quilts and covers can be viewed as optional extras in the interior, accessories rather than essentials. But where finishes and surfaces are hard as opposed to yielding, such details supply a necessary dimension of comfort, both practical and aesthetic. Soft furnishings only tend to look redundant and self-indulgent where rooms are already carpeted, swathed and padded. In more sparse or hard-edged surroundings, the casual informality of a pile of cushions or a softening quilt introduces warmth and a human touch. If the rest of the room is fairly neutral and restrained, colourful detail in the form of accessories can inject a welcome note of vitality. These furnishings also tend to be cheap, which makes change affordable.

Soft furnishings provide the opportunity to be more exuberant with colour. Natural dyes are anything but unassuming. Vibrant ochres, mustards, sage and moss greens, deep blush madder and damson, and soothing indigo are increasingly replacing the sterile primary shades of synthetic chemical colour as major retailers discover the power of these traditionally produced dyes. There is almost no combination which won't work together, which means that accessories can be added or subtracted without having to change the basic scheme of a room.

Naturally dyed linens and cottons are the staple fabrics of ethnic cushion covers, throws and woven blankets. The searing colours can be further emphasized by adding traditional hand-quilting, blanket stitching or figurative embroidery. Bandhini textiles, for example, from Rajasthan, are traditional sun-bleached tie-dye fabrics with a puckered surface which adds a textural dimension. Mud- or wax-resist patterns are traditional forms of fabric decoration in India and the Far East. The irregularity of these prints, where you can almost sense the press of the printer's block, is part of their appeal.

Since soft furnishing accessories are relatively inexpensive – even more so if you make them yourself – you can vary the way you dress a room to respond to the different moods of the seasons. Substituting lightweight cotton throws for blankets in warm rich colours instantly gives a room a summery look.

This simple strategy can be taken further by exchanging dark-toned loose (slip) covers on upholstered chairs and sofas for paler versions in the brighter months. Loose covers in general make better practical sense than close tailored upholstery, for the obvious reason that they can be removed easily for washing or cleaning and renewed fairly cheaply once they have worn out. Many upholstered pieces are also available as a basic natural calico cover, a raw unfinished look that can be very appealing. Instant natural covers can also be improvized by draping fabric, bed sheets, spreads or quilts over a sofa or chair.

For bed linen natural materials offer the ultimate in comfort in bed. Choose crisp cotton and linen for sheets and pillowcases which lie next to the skin, wool or flannel for blankets to provide a cosy enveloping warmth; down or feather-filled duvets and pillows for basic bedding. Layers of bright quilts, fringed throws or vibrantly patterned bedspreads serve to play up the bed's importance; all-white linen is timelessly elegant, cool and refreshing. You can also dress a bed with curtains or drapery.

Boldly striped canvas, attached by means of simple tabs to a wooden rod, creates a swaying hammock, a breezy addition to a rural garden. A director's chair receives similarly graphic treatment. (LEFT).

Injecting colour and pattern into a naturally decorated room is most easily done with soft furnishings such as throws and cushions. Bows and tassels sewn on to simple linen or calico cushions add decorative interest and light relief in otherwise unfussy rooms (ABOVE).

A plain wooden or metal framework provides a perfect basis for hanging loose folds of muslin, tropical-style, or suspending simple curtains from ties, tapes or loops.

Lighting

Natural light changes from hour to hour, day to day; it is rarely static in tone, level, intensity or colour. These variations may be almost imperceptible but they seem in some profound way to be tied to our sense of well-being. The purpose of artificial light is to stand in for daylight at night-time or in the darker times of the year. But in many homes artificial light is anything but subtle in its effect. Glaring overhead fittings often emit dazzling illumination that is tiring and monotonous. Unshielded bulbs strain the eyes, and poorly placed or ill-chosen light sources and fittings alter the perception of colour and cast a sickly glow. Interior lighting that is not designed to imitate the subtlety of

Cerulean blue walls and blue and white natural fabrics are a clean and classic colour combination (FAR LEFT).

The cool texture of linen against the skin makes it ideal for sheets and bedding. Slate blue and grey make an elegant colour scheme for a Scandinavian bedhead (LEFT).

A low bed placed at window height in a sparsely furnished room is the ideal location for deep sleep. For further security and peace of mind, giant cotton bed drapes and curtains exclude the view at night-time (ABOVE).

natural light can never enhance the comfort or atmosphere of a room.

When you are choosing lighting, one important factor to consider is the quality of the light source. Tungsten bulbs, still the most common source of domestic light, cast a warm yellowish glow. Fluorescent light, on the other hand, is greenish, which gives it a cold appearance. Compact fluorescent lamps also give out a cold light but are long-lasting and energy efficient. Tungsten-halogen lamps emit a sparkling white light that is closest to daylight. Low-voltage halogen lamps, often used in accent lighting, are also among the most energy efficient. Fittings are smaller, less heat is emitted and lamps, though expensive, have an incredibly long life.

Lighting schemes should be devised to support the activities that take place in each room, balancing atmosphere and mood with functional requirements. A central pendant in every area might well supply adequate light for most needs, but there is no surer way of divesting a room of character and interest. By contrast, providing a number of different light sources, varying in direction and level of intensity, creates overlapping pools of light that is instinctively more pleasing. Background lighting can be supplied by means of a variety of individual sources, which together raise the general level of illumination without creating hard shadows or a uniform glare. Table lamps, uplights, downlights, spots and side lights can be positioned or angled to bounce light off walls and ceilings and avoid the need for a single fixed source. Task lights, which focus bright light in a single direction, are required for places such as desks, kitchen worktops or study areas where concentrated work takes place. Accent light, which need not be very bright, is extremely useful for

picking out points of decorative or architectural interest.

The quality of a light source can also be dramatically affected by the fitting or shade which shields it. Paper, silk and parchment softly diffuse the light; metal shades and fittings create a more directional, hard-edged effect. A wide variety of light fittings and fixtures that will enhance natural-style decoration are produced nowadays, from the ubiquitous paper lantern shade to table lamps with

Exposed brick walls and generous amounts of natural daylight combine to enhance the curving architectural lines of a converted warehouse (LEFT).

Rough-hewn slate is used judiciously as a splashback around bath and sink, while an ingenious light fitting fashioned from a fallen branch and old stones provides a witty counterpoint in this elemental bathroom (ABOVE).

roughcast earthenware bases and parchment shades. In addition to the standard globes, paper lanterns come in a variety of sizes and organic, cocoon-like shapes, as well as in natural unbleached paper stiffened with bamboo. Japanese-style paper lamps on metal stands, reminiscent of Noguchi designs, make delightful bedside or table lamps. Metal shades come pierced with spots and stars, in enamelled colours, ungalvanized finishes and a range of circumferences. Clip-on aluminium loft lights have a basic aesthetic which suits many different situations, as do floor-standing photographer's lights with interchangeable metal shades.

Artificial light should be seen as the partner of daylight, rather than its absolute substitute. You can maximize the amount of natural light a room receives and therefore reduce your reliance on artificial sources by decorating in pale or neutral colours, so that light is bounced off and reflected from surfaces and finishes.

Mirrors are another useful ally. In the past, precious and expensive candlelight was multiplied by the reflective sheen of mirror-backed sconces and mirror-lined walls; nowadays the need may not be as acute, but the impact of a carefully placed mirror can be just as effective. Place a mirror where it will catch the light from a window, reflect a beautiful view or introduce a sense of spaciousness. One really good location is opposite an entrance way; such a position creates interior vistas which seem to dissolve solid walls and partitions. Large mirrors have an inherent impact but even smaller mirrors add a sparkling quality to interior lighting.

Dimmer switches allow you to adjust light levels to a fine degree, to suit the mood or needs of the moment.

The best way of making light work naturally in a living room is to use a combination of ceiling, wall and table lamps which will vary the intensity of the light according to mood and need. Sometimes candles alone will suffice if you are simply relaxing in the room. For reading, use table lamps fitted with paper or metal shades and dot them around your main seating area. Create mood by switching on several table lamps, an uplighter or two and a low-wattage wall or recessed ceiling light.

RAFFIA FRINGED CUSHION

Cushions make good accent points in a decorative scheme and are easy to interchange with other soft furnishings. Natural fabrics and trimmings are cheap and widely available. When combining heavy and light fabrics, back patches of light, translucent fabrics such as muslin with a strong, close-weave cotton.

Suitable fabrics for simply made natural cushions include calico, rough-weave linen, hessian (burlap), cotton damask, silk taffeta, vegetable-dyed linen and woven raffia. They all blend well with natural materials such as bleached wooden floorboards or cane and rattan furniture. Simple woven raffia matting used as fringing adds textural interest to these buttoned-gingham cushion covers, while a complete cover of woven matting can be given an extra dimension with the addition of personalized name tapes. Matting can be replaced with fringed jute or hessian fringing.

MATERIALS

Square cushion pad,
    30 x 30cm (12 x 12in)
Blue gingham fabric
Raffia matting
White sewing thread
Two white buttons,
    2.5cm(1in) diameter
Chalk or marker pen
Scissors

MEASURING UP

For the front of the cushion, cut one square of fabric 30 x 30cm (12 x 12in) plus 1.25cm (½in) to allow for the seam allowances on all sides.

For the back of the cushion, cut two rectangles of fabric 30 x 15cm (12 x 6in), one with 1.25cm (½in) seam allowances on all sides and one with 1.25cm (½in) allowances on three sides and a 6cm (2½in) allowance on the fourth side for buttonholes. Cut two strips of raffia matting, each 32.5 x 8.75cm (13 x 3½in) with a seam allowance of 1.25cm (½in). Then fray the ends to form a fringe.

METHOD

1 To make up the back of the cushion, lay the fabric rectangle with the buttonhole allowance and lay it right side down. Turn under a 2.5cm (1in) side turning along the remaining raw edge, followed by a 3.5cm(1½in) hem. Machine-stitch and press. Machine- or handsew two vertical button holes, each 2.5cm (1in) wide. These should be positioned 10cm (4in) in from the top and bottom edges.

2 Place the other fabric rectangle right side down. Make a double 60mm (⅛in) turning along the left-hand raw edge. Machine-stitch and press. Mark the position of the buttons, then sew them in place. Place this rectangle, right side down, alongside the first and overlapping it by 3.5cm (1½in), so that the buttonholes cover the buttons. Pin in position. Sew the two rectangles together at both ends of the vertical vent, 5cm (2in) in from the edge, and along the inner edge of the buttonholed vent for added strength (see 4).

3 Take the large square of fabric for the front of the cushion and place it right side up. Next, place the raffia along each side, with the fringing facing inwards. Pin the raffia in position.

4 Place the vented back square of fabric right side down onto the front square, so that the raffia is sandwiched in between. Pin in position. Machine-stitch around all four sides with a seam allowance of 1.5cm (½in) to form the cushion casing. Clip all four corners. Turn the casing right side out. Press.

1

2

3

4

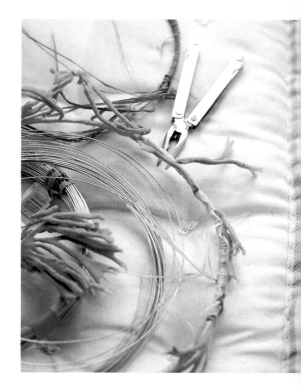

DISPLAY

DISPLAY

Display is the foreground of the interior. Whatever you put on show inevitably takes pride of place, attracting and holding the attention to a far greater degree than the basic elements of surfaces and finishes. Rooms without pictures, flowers or decorative objects of any kind can be beautiful spaces, but they seem to lack a flavour, a sense of being inhabited. Displays that reflect the personal tastes and pleasures of the people who create them are more than mere finishing touches; they provide a room with its essence and focus.

A display can amuse, startle, astonish, impress or delight; the only rule is surround yourself with things that mean something to you. If pictures that occupy wall space or objects that perch on mantelpieces have little more to recommend them than the fact that they are safe and inoffensive, the overall effect will have no more personality than a tasteful hotel room.

Natural displays breathe life into a room. Fresh flowers are one of the most obvious and certainly the most common of ways to bring nature indoors. Souvenirs of country walks or seaside strolls can be equally evocative, and more long-lasting. The scope is boundless; ingredients are plentiful and free. Shells, weathered wood, seed pods and beachstones can all be collected and provide an eloquent summary of the textures, colours and patterns of natural decorating.

Natural displays also offer the opportunity to ring the changes, and respond to the different moods of the seasons. All they require is a favourable position, where light reveals the play of texture and surface. Unlike fixed or artfully formal effects, the fluidity of these spontaneous arrangements provides yet another means of bringing vitality and beauty to our surroundings.

Natural displays place the emphasis very much on textural contrast. The delicacy of white flowerheads *is effectively set off by weathered metal containers, smooth beachstones and slatted table top* (ABOVE). *Found objects can form an integral part of any natural display. A rugged frame constructed of* *flotsam and jetsam echoes the rough texture of battered whitewashed plasterwork* (RIGHT).

impulse to find the perfect seashell, the largest limpet or the most sculpturally contorted branch.

Natural displays help to preserve the memory of such irresistible discoveries. In surroundings which are themselves decorated and furnished to evoke the natural world, these poignant reminders of forays on the seashore or in the countryside take on a particular meaning and relevance.

You don't have to go to a great deal of trouble to arrange your finds – in fact, the least trouble the better. Large smooth stones can also do duty as paperweights or doorstops, as hearth-side guardians, stacked in a cairn on a shelf or as a miniature shingled beach around a floor-level lamp. Shells find a natural home in the watery world of the bathroom, ranged along windowsills, packed into clear glass containers or displayed specimen-fashion on top of a chest of drawers. Knarled twists of driftwood transform a mantelpiece into a plinth for sculpture.

The art of found objects

Natural treasures, such as seashells, stones and driftwood, can be bought but that somehow misses the point. The joy of discovery, one of the earliest and most enduring of life's pleasures, gives found objects their special meaning. Knowing on which beach or in which wood you unearthed your prize underscores the delight of such trophies. Many people return from holiday or weekend breaks with pockets and rucksacks stuffed with 'finds'. Instead of simply discarding such mementoes, you can easily incorporate them into your surroundings and relish the elemental qualities and associations they offer.

Children tend to be unselfconscious and rather random in their pickings. But as we sift the detritus on the beach, or crunch through crisp autumn leaves on a bridlepath, we may indulge in a more selective attitude. The eye may be entranced by smooth pebbles graphically bisected with stripes of quartz, or stones worn by erosion into Henry Moore look-alikes, pierced with holes. We may scout the shoreline for bits of flotsam and jetsam, fragments of weathered wood, with curls of flaking paint still adhering to their softened contours. We may be driven by an

A simple harmony of textures is the basis for this display. Pottery urns and driftwood complement the rubbed, distressed finish of the junkshop cupboard and the patchy colours of the painting (FAR LEFT).

A beachcomber's treasure trove provides an endless source of inspiration. Found objects need little in the way of arrangement; the simpler the display, the better (TOP LEFT).

Elements can be informally combined in a variety of ways to bring a sense of vitality to the interior. Grouping objects near windows highlights textural contrast (LEFT).

Flowers, foliage and plants

Flowers are the one natural element that virtually everybody has in the home at one time or another. Even so, some flowers might be said to be more natural than others. In recent years, floral fashion has swung away from the stiff, rather formal arrangements of perfect hothouse blooms embedded in foam, in favour of the type of loose unstructured displays that recall the informality of the cottage garden. Like the cottage garden, these arrangements may include fruit, berries, vegetables or almost anything else that grows.

Fresh flowers appear at their most natural when they are both seasonal and local. The horticultural industry has grown in sophistication in recent years, supplying florists with novelties such as exotic flora flown in from tropical climes, spring flowers in the depths of winter and the most popular flowers all the year round. With constant availability, flowers can lose their associations. The first sight of snowdrops

*Flowers provide
an immediate
connection with the
world of nature.
Summer blooms
massed in front of
an antique mirror
recreate the
abundance of the
cottage garden
(FAR LEFT).*

*Purple alium on long
spindly stems echo the
spare lines of
metalwork figures
and a row of
horseshoes
(CENTRE LEFT).*

*Meadow flowers in
weathered canisters
bring a breath of
country air indoors
(LEFT).*

*Sunflowers and
ripening gourds
suggest the bounty
of harvest (BELOW).*

just as winter is beginning to lessen its grip, the luscious heady blooms of early summer, the dusky tints of Michaelmas daisies at the end of the year echo the progress of the seasons making their appearance all the more welcome. The added bonus of the seasonal approach is that flowers that have not been cultivated outside their natural growing period are often cheaper, so you can afford more of them, more often.

Twigs and branches, ivy and other evergreen foliage, winter berries, pine cones, seed pods and autumn leaves widen the scope still further; much of this material can be collected from the garden or brought home from country walks for free, but it goes without saying that picking wild flowers or cutting branches and fresh foliage in parks or woodland is nothing less than vandalism and in some areas may be strictly illegal.

Dried flowers and seed pods have always provided a source of material for natural displays during the lean times of the year, when the garden is dormant.

Some dried flowers, however, can look curiously artificial; the ubiquitous bunches of statice and everlasting seem no more natural than plastic or silk flowers. Others are more evocative. Dried rose heads, lavender or hydrangeas – whose papery petals and subtle faded colours can be even more beautiful than their fresh counterparts – can be massed in tight clusters for midwinter displays. Seed cases, such as poppy heads or eucalyptus pods, also make effective arrangements.

Choose containers for flowers and foliage that will enhance the natural theme. Containers can be improvized from a wide variety of different objects; they don't necessarily even need to be waterproof. Flowers can be arranged in water-filled jars that are then placed inside baskets, unglazed terracotta pottery, flower pots, wooden trays, trugs or lacquer boxes. Galvanized buckets and watering cans provide a witty contrast for delicate white flowers.

House plants demand a thorough-going approach to avoid seeming like poor relations of their garden cousins. Small- to medium-sized plants, like objects, often look more attractive grouped, arranged on metal garden shelving or on a sunny south-facing sill where they can take on the aspect of an indoor garden.

Just as a lone shrub in a border, planted in splendid isolation, would look decidedly ill-at-ease, you should arrange indoor plants with some attention to basic composition and compatibility. In temperate zones, tender plants such as herbs, scented-leaf geraniums, ficus, streptocarpus and various species of fern somehow look more at home and therefore more natural than the more obviously exotic or tropical species, which can often import an somewhat alien quality to the interior.

Decorative arrangements

Because it crowns the hearth, the traditional focus of the home, the mantelpiece has become the classic domestic shrine, the repository for flowers, memorabilia and decorative objects of all kinds. The mantelpiece is also conveniently at eye-level, which gives added emphasis and visibility to what you place there. The hearth itself can also provide a good place for display. Large African baskets, crusty terracotta urns or abundant displays of berried branches, flowers or foliage can stand in place of a real fire. It is important to get the scale right – puny arrangements at floor level will just look lost.

Other good locations for display include windowsills, shelves and tabletops. The windowsill is the ideal site for objects that are enhanced by light, such as coloured glass, antique bottles and leaded glass panels. Recycled glass has a beautiful rippled quality that is accentuated by backlighting.

Display areas often work more effectively when collections are grouped according to a theme. Play colour against colour, texture against texture, or assemble objects with a common denominator of provenance, type or material. Experiment with different arrangements and locations to keep the effect fresh and lively.

The Japanese notion of display relies on the eloquent impact of a single sparse arrangement of flowers, an artefact or a painting in an otherwise empty room. Recesses or alcoves are traditionally the places designated for these visual shrines. By varying what is displayed, exchanging a ceramic bowl for a few flowering branches for instance, the sense of beauty is never dulled.

Even if Western rooms are not as minimal as Japanese interiors, by rotating objects in and out of prominence – even

Moody blue provides the common denominator for this window-scape. Colour is one of the easiest themes for displays, uniting elements as diverse as flowers, plates and curtains (LEFT).

Wood salvaged from the seashore makes evocative natural frames. Groups of similar objects, pictures or flowers have much more impact than individual items dotted about a room (ABOVE).

retiring some out of sight for a while – we can heighten our appreciation of what is on view. Another way of keeping perceptions sharp is to site displays in hallways, on landings or in other places of transition, where they may be glimpsed but not lingered over and thus will retain their ability to delight.

Less can also be more when it comes to annexing wall space for display. Densely hung rows of pictures and prints need not be ruled out, but they require plenty of surrounding breathing space to avoid a claustrophobic effect. Line drawings, black-and-white prints and photographs have an elegant, understated quality that works well with natural decorating. Maps and sea charts lend graphic interest; overscale lithographs featuring blocks of vibrant colour sing out against pale backgrounds and enliven cool or neutral settings. For a more sculptural effect, you can hang hats, baskets, masks or fabric on the walls, or frame up collages of natural specimens in glass-fronted box frames.

For conveying a natural mood, the frame can be almost as important as the picture or object it displays. Improvized frames of corrugated cardboard, pieces of weathered planking or driftwood, mosaic or mirror glass, punched tin or beaten metal provide a change from the standard painted, stained or varnished wooden frame. Look out for interesting frames surrounding discardable art in junkshops or fleamarkets – this sort of approach is much cheaper and more original than relying on what is generally available from picture framers.

Celebrations

Any celebration offers an excuse to change gear and heighten the sense of drama and theatricality in the interior. Aside from such seasonal markers as Christmas, New Year and Easter, other occasions provide an opportunity to pull out all the stops. Birthdays, dinner parties, weddings and family gatherings deserve some kind of special effort in terms of decoration and display.

For a natural Christmas, deck the tree with pungent cinnamon sticks, citrus fruit stuck with cloves, gingerbread biscuits, star anise, twists of raffia or scrim. You can buy living trees grown in pots, which can be replanted in the garden, or invest in a twiggy tree made of trimmed branches nailed to a central post to bring out year after year. If you

Odd corners out of
eyeline can be highly
effective locations for
arrangements. The
cool whitewashed
contours of a cottage
doorframe provide
just the right spot for
a collection of
majolica bowls
(FAR LEFT).

Metalwork,
porcelain, stoneware
and carved wood
come together on a
table top for a display
with an Eastern
influence. The paper
lantern
on metal legs,
reminiscent of a
Noguchi design,
is a contemporary
classic (LEFT).

prefer the traditional cut spruce there are recycling centres where trees can be pulped into bark chippings for garden use after Christmas is over.

Natural wrapping materials include recycled paper, ordinary brown wrapping paper customized by sponge or potato printing, coloured newsprint and swathes of gauze, net or muslin. Tie up parcels with scrim, raffia, garden twine or string and decorate with seed pods, pine cones, sprigs of holly or leaf tags.

The table is the focus for many celebrations. For a tablecloth, it is hard to improve upon classic white damask, but covers can also be improvized from craft paper, secured to the underside of the table with masking tape, or lengths of any inexpensive fabric, such as calico or muslin. You can dye such materials very easily at home, or decorate with fabric paints.

Seasonal fruit and vegetables heaped in gaily coloured ceramic bowls or piled on platters or leaf plates make appetizing centrepieces. Lemons arranged in an indigo earthenware bowl, limes laid in a metal mesh basket or glossy purple-skinned aubergines (eggplants) on a carved wooden platter provide a celebratory jolt of colour equal to the most extravagant flower arrangement.

Soft, flickering candlelight turns any event into a special occasion. Church candles come in a wide variety of heights and widths; beeswax candles delicately scent the air. Shallow nightlights can be floated in water-filled bowls or placed in the bottom of coloured glasses to make instant garden lanterns.

Everyday things

Display, in one sense, can be just what happens to be on view. The necessities of life – wastepaper bins, laundry baskets, scrubbing brushes, kitchen utensils, handles and catches, can't always be

Fruit and vegetables make appetizing displays. Oranges piled high in a terracotta bowl glazed in searing yellow provide a jolt of colour (LEFT).

Colourful lemons and limes suspended from loops of gauzy ribbon ring the changes on the traditional glass Christmas baubles (ABOVE).

Recycled paper, embedded with stalks, petals and leaf fragments, makes evocative wrapping paper. For natural packaging, try nestling presents in crisp autumn leaves bedded in a recycled cardboard box (RIGHT).

The flickering glow of candlelight makes a welcome sight on a winter's evening. Candles, like other objects, gain impact when massed or grouped together (ABOVE).

Natural decorating directs attention to everyday objects (RIGHT).

hidden from sight. But if these household basics are good-looking, there is no real reason for concealment.

It is on this common or garden level that synthetic materials are most typically and intrusively evident in the home. But by making a few simple substitutions, you can extend the natural aesthetic to the ordinary things you need and use every day. Old-fashioned hardware stores are good sources for enamelled or galvanized buckets, basins and watering cans; wood and bristle brushes, besom brooms, and terracotta plant pots. Wooden clothes horses, wicker laundry baskets and bins are handsome as well as practical. In the bathroom, marine sponges, pumice stones and loofahs are traditional natural accompaniments to bathing. Metal or porcelain switch plates, door handles and other such details are infinitely more sympathetic than their plastic counterparts.

Storage containers for organizing paperwork, tools or other items include simple stacking boxes, drawers and pigeonholes in recycled and recyclable cardboard, galvanized metal or untreated pine. Versatile and anonymous, these containers work as well in living rooms and bedrooms as in studies, studios or workshops. Foodstuffs can be decanted into decorative jars, metal canisters or earthenware crocks. Empty cans, with the labels soaked off, can be recycled as useful homes for pencils, pens and brushes. Tools and equipment in regular use can be hung from wire racks, metal rails or peg boards for homely yet practical displays.

Wearing well and serving well, ordinary things bring the natural approach to the heart of everyday life.

Hardware stores or old-fashioned ironmongers can be a very good source of traditional household goods, such as galvanized pails and watering cans, besom brooms and bristle brushes, enamelled basins, jugs and bowls (RIGHT).

WALL CUPBOARD

Old metal first-aid cabinets, aluminium tin cans, zinc chests or even filing cabinets, wall-mounted or freestanding, can be given a parchment-effect surface decoration using plain lining paper. The cabinet we used here was originally a bright red lacquered metal. The finished effect is an attractive scumbled surface which can be applied to produce naturally aged surfaces in any room.

MATERIALS

Old metal cabinet
Lining paper (enough to cover the
    surface area of your cupboard twice)
Water-based white emulsion (latex)
2 shades of brown emulsion (latex)
    (one dark, one light)
5cm (2in) paintbrush
Wallpaper paste
Proprietary wall filler
Plaster of Paris
Water

PREPARATION

Wash the cabinet and dry thoroughly. Sand the cabinet to give it a key.

METHOD

1 Using wallpaper paste, stick small pieces of lining paper over the entire surface area of the cabinet so that they overlap, creating a mottled effect.

2 When the paste has dried, paint the cabinet with the paler shade of brown emulsion, mixed with a little wall filler. Leave it to dry. Then apply a skim of plaster of Paris over the entire surface.

3 Mix the second, darker shade of brown emulsion with wall filler to make a thin paste, apply a smooth coat and allow to dry. When it has hardened, sand the surface in patches so that layers of paint show through to give a crumbling, aged patina.

1

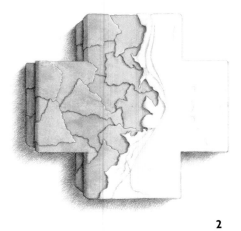

2

3

PLASTERCAST OBJECTS

Plastercasts of everyday objects make intriguing decorations for a mantel shelf or window ledge, or they can be hung on the wall. Place them near light sources for dramatic effect and group two or three casts together to lend coherence to a wall or floor display. In bathrooms lean them on surfaces where you have boxed in pipes. For the best effects, choose objects with strong, simple shapes.

MATERIALS

Display object (such as a bottle, glass or spoon)
4 pieces of scrap board
Masking tape
Plasticine
Two-part catalytic rubber mould-making liquid (from craft or hobby shops)
Plaster of Paris

METHOD

1 Mount your chosen object and press it firmly into a bed of Plasticine. If it is hollow, fill it with Plasticine so that a 'positive', or solid, image can be made.

2 Tape together the 4 wooden boards, which should be both deeper than the object and approximately 2.5–5cm (1–2in) larger than the object on all sides.

3 Place the object, complete with Plasticine base, into the wooden frame. Pour the two-part catalytic rubber mould-making liquid into the frame so that the object is covered and the frame is filled. (The liquid sets quickly and so should not leak out, but a tray can be placed beneath it for safety.) Leave for about 30 minutes to set; then remove the object from the frame.

4 You now have a rubber 'negative', or mould. Fill this with plaster of Paris and leave to set for a further 30 minutes. Remove the plaster cast from the mould.

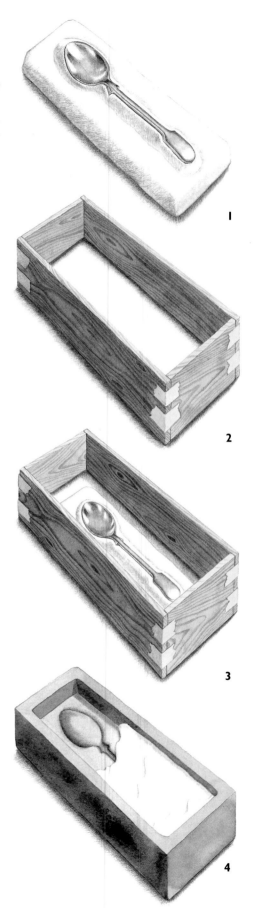

1

2

3

4

SEAWEED WREATH

A decorating classic, wreaths have a long tradition of use in the home and also a symbolic significance, representing the 'circle of life' in a variety of different forms. This seaweed wreath is quick and easy to make. Look for different kinds of seaweed on the seashore and introduce different textures and tones: greens, ochres and tawny browns.

If you do not have access to the seashore, try making a wreath from discarded natural materials. Use gilded oak leaves or sprayed dried seed pods, feathers, or sun-bleached twigs to make good use of nature's cast-offs.

MATERIALS
Medium-thickness florist's wire
Wire cutters
Dried seaweed
Raffia

METHOD

1 Using wire cutters, cut 4 or 5 lengths of medium-thickness florist's wire to form a circle about 10in (25cm) in diameter. Bind them together at intervals with 4 shorter lengths to add strength and stiffness.

2 Twist the seaweed stems through the wire to anchor them, then bind them tightly in place around the wire circle, using overlapping lengths of raffia, until the wire is covered.

3 Additional short lengths of raffia can be used to make the seaweed still more secure if necessary. Tie on an extra strip of raffia from which to hang the wreath. Alternatively, simply suspend it from a picture hook in a bathroom, bedroom or living room.

1

2

3

THE ECO-FRIENDLY INTERIOR

There are countless ways of living a more environmentally friendly existence without evangelically setting out to change your lifestyle overnight. Start off gently, and over time you may realize that it is actually quite easy to adopt ecological attitudes to decorating and furnishing your home. Once you have made a few adjustments you will find increased enjoyment in natural alternatives to artifice, conspicuous consumption and waste.

RECYCLING

Never use new materials when old ones can be recycled. In decorating terms, investigate the re-use of raw materials for new furniture and furnishing schemes. Always re-use wood, fabric and paper around the house whenever possible.

Provide yourself with the means of recycling newspaper, glass, tins, plastic bottles and food waste. Try to set aside a small area of the kitchen or a space outside for this purpose. There are a wide range of bins available on the market nowadays specifically for glass or tin, as well as for storing compost internally. Alternatively, you can customize your own containers.

USING NATURAL MATERIALS

Choosing decorating products

The subject of eco-friendly paints, stains, varnishes, wallpaper adhesives and primers is one which is fraught with confusion and misinformation. However, a small but increasing number of companies are prepared to declare the ingredients of their products. Whenever possible, use products whose provenance and ingredients are listed on the packaging, and beware of anything wrapped in brown paper packaging bearing words such as 'Environmentally Friendly': sometimes this may not tell the whole story.

Wood

Many individual furniture makers use reclaimed timber whenever possible, ranging from wood from storm-damaged trees several centuries old to Victorian pine floorboards and furniture from defunct schools, houses and churches. (See page 138 for more information on environmentally acceptable woods.)

Paper

Wallpapers, lampshades and stationery made of recycled paper are becoming increasingly available as consumers demand environmentally friendly goods. Recycled paper can be used to make decorative papier-mâché objects and as a wall covering (see page 38), while recycled paper lampshades cast a soft, yellow light.

Matting versus carpet

Coir, seagrass, sisal and jute are all natural floor coverings that can be used instead of carpets. Unless they are made of pure wool and untreated, carpets usually incorporate harmful irritants in their backing, and many are routinely treated with insecticides; even pure wool

carpets are sometimes treated with a mothproofing agent that contains toxic petrochemicals. Choose one hundred per cent untreated wool carpets if matting is unacceptable.

WALLS

Choosing natural paints and stains

With the growing awareness that oil- (solvent-) based paints, manufactured from petrochemicals are toxic, there has been a flood of new 'environmentally friendly' paints and related products available on the market. However, the distinctions between tradition, historically authentic and ecologically sound have become blurred, with a few companies claiming that products are safe to use because they were the norm a couple of hundred years ago.

Traditional does not necessarily mean safe. Some clarification may be helpful here. All paints comprise a pigment (colourant), a binding agent (which helps the colourant adhere to the surface), and a solvent (which keeps the paint in suspension until it is ready to be used). The main difference between organic and non-organic paint

is usually the ingredient used as the solvent. Oil-based paints contain non-renewable and toxic petrochemicals, while water-based paints contain naturally occurring plant and vegetable oils that are equally effective.

Water-based paints

These are used on interior walls. Water-based emulsion can be watered down, about two parts paint to one part water, to create a wash for walls or furniture. Seal the wash with a natural varnish (see right). Alternatively, you can leave it untreated for a more informal finish. A few companies now produce water-based gloss and eggshell (lustre) paints as well as emulsion (latex). (See Sources for a list of stockists.)

Oil-(solvent-) based paint

Usually known as gloss or eggshell, this is an effective paint for covering both interior and exterior woodwork, but it is a toxic product made from non-renewable sources. Opt instead for ecologically sound paints based on linseed oil or, if you do choose oil-based paints, use them sparingly and always in well-ventilated environments.

Distemper

A traditional wall treatment, distemper is the current darling of professional decorators. Although it is ecologically sound – it is made primarily from chalk and water – its main drawbacks are that it is not washable, will not adhere to walls that have already been painted and cannot be painted over with emulsion. It does, however, allow walls to breathe, so is best used on newly plastered walls. Another reason why this traditional product is enjoying a revival, despite its disadvantages, is that with the addition of artists' oil paints or other pigments, distemper takes on rich, textural, chalky colours that are unlike any commercially prepared emulsion. (See page 36 for distemper recipe.)

Casein paints

These are water-based paints that contain casein (a milk protein), which gives a matt, textured finish to both wood and walls. Casein paints are environmentally friendly.

Limewash

Also know as whitewash, real limewash is perhaps one of the most misunderstood of the 'traditional' wall finishes. Made from slaked lime (calcium hydroxide) and water, its advantages are that it allows walls to breathe and creates a delightful matt finish that can be further enhanced by the addition of coloured pigments. On the downside, though, limewash is caustic, can only be applied to bare plaster and cannot be painted over synthetic paints. It is best suited to exterior or interior walls that need to breathe. If applied to damp walls, salt deposits are likely to gather on the surface. Several manufacturers produce a commercial limewash that is less caustic than the traditional recipe (see Sources for details).

WINDOWS AND DOORS

Natural varnishes

Good alternatives to the vapour-producing polyurethane varnishes are organic varnishes based on natural resins, such as larch or copal, combined with natural turpentine oil and pigments. Amber can also be used; it produces a deep lustre and wears well.

Shellac is a natural resin produced by the lac insect of India and the Far East. It creates a thin lacquer that can be used as a safe varnish for wooden furniture. A coat of shellac will inhibit the escape of fumes from particleboard and MDF (medium-density fibreboard).

Linseed oil is a pale yellow natural by-product of flax and forms the basis for many natural varnishes. When combined with turpentine oil it can be used to make organic gloss paint. It is also to be found in furniture polish.

Natural wax

Keep wood lustrous and rich-looking by regular seasoning with beeswax. A wholly natural material, it will protect new and restored wood used internally, whether furniture, doors or floors.

Natural wood stains

These are based on natural resins and are applied by painting on a neutral base coat, allowing it to dry, and then applying a top coat to which a stain concentrate has been added.

Natural thinners

These contain pure plant oils such as citrus peel and pine, and can be used for cleaning brushes or for thinning stains, waxes, varnish, primers and oil paints.

ECO-FRIENDLY WOOD

Choosing wood

The main criteria to use when you are choosing new wood for the home are Check Your Sources and Think Local. Timber that is acquired from properly managed, sustainable forests will always be replaced as it is felled, and indigenous timber will involve cheaper transportation costs and, therefore, less energy expenditure. When buying any kind of wood, check its provenance with your supplier.

Some hardwoods, such as European and North American oak, ash, beech, poplar, maple and walnut, are sustainably managed and are suitable for external joinery in addition to the cheaper softwoods. However, try to avoid tropical hardwoods, such as Indonesian teak and African and Brazilian mahogany, which are impossible to replenish quickly and whose felling involves further destruction of already endangered rainforests.

Sustainable and plentiful softwoods include fir, spruce, larch, pine and deal (a low-grade form of pine). Softwoods are most often used for furniture and interior woodwork. They are easy to work with and hardwearing when protected with a layer of organic paint, varnish or stain.

Using wood

Wood used decoratively around the home is both hardwearing and homely. Tongue-and-groove boarding applied as cladding in hallways, living rooms, kitchens and bathrooms creates an instant sense of enclosure. Not only can it conceal ugly pipework or uneven plaster, but it is also a strong decorative device in its own right.

Wood alternatives

Wood alternatives include cane and grasses, such as bamboo and rattan; like tropical hardwoods, these materials have been over-exploited in recent years so, whenever possible, check that new cane and rattan furniture comes from managed sources. Limit as much as possible your use of the cheaper wood alternatives, such as particleboard and MDF (medium-density fibreboard) because these composite materials, made up from scraps of wood and fibres, are bound together with various toxic resins such as formaldehyde, a known carcinogen that emits poisonous vapours. You can minimize its harmful effects by applying a non-toxic paint and/or varnish to the bare board.

DYEING AND PRINTING NATURAL FABRIC

A way of injecting colour into a natural scheme is to dye your own fabric or yarns using plant and vegetable dyes, whose soft, luminous tones are hard to emulate in commercially dyed fabrics.

Fabrics for dyeing

Try dyeing a small area of fabric first to check for consistency of colour. Experiment with cheaper fabrics, such as muslin and unbleached cotton. Then move on to more luxurious materials, such as linen and silk. For bold curtains, try tie-dye or batik motifs in vivid ochres and terracottas.

Plant and vegetable dyes

The following colours can be effectively obtained from using the corresponding plants and vegetables:
Fuchsia: cochineal
Burgundy: Brazilwood chips
Blue: woad leaves
    (from the wild plant *Isatis tinctoria*)
Green: weld (from *Reseda luteola*,
    commonly known as Dyer's Rocket)

DYEING METHODS

Batik

Batik is an Indonesian resist-dyeing technique using a mixture of wax, resin, oil, paraffin, rice and bean paste or mud, which is applied to areas of the fabric where the dye is not intended to penetrate. When the dyeing is finished, the resist is washed out. Batik templates can be decorative objects in their own right. Similar techniques are used for African adinkre cloth.

Tie-dyeing

Tie-dying is a form of resist-dyeing in which areas of a fabric not to be coloured are tied or knotted in order to escape the dye.

Yarn-dyeing

Yarn-dying is a method of dyeing yarn before it is woven or sewn into a fabric.

Ikat

Ikat is a process whereby either the warp or weft of a fabric is tie-dyed before weaving to create a distinctive pattern.

PRESERVING AND DISPLAYING NATURAL COLLECTIONS

Shelving

Naive-style wall-mounted shelves can be made from reclaimed timber such as old floorboards or driftwood. Paint them with a colourwash of off-white or chalky blue and place on them your favourite items of flotsam and jetsam.

Dried flowers, seed heads and grasses

Allow the delicate heads of roses and hydrangeas to dry naturally and arrange the cut flowers loosely in a clear glass vase on a window ledge to catch the light. Alternatively, place them in front of a paper-shaded table lamp to show off their natural textures. Seed heads, such as those of cow parsley, honesty, poppies, grasses, barley and wheat, exquisitely varied in their shapes, textures and neutral shades, look perfect in a white or cream interior scheme.

Treasure trove

Country and seaside walks can yield all manner of strange and beautiful objects discarded by man or nature: sculptural branches and twigs, pine cones, unusual leaves, seaweed, old chandlers' rope, stones, starfish and seashells can all be transformed into attractive and original decorative objects and they will harmonize well with a natural scheme. Once home, arrange your finds to make an informal collection in a clear container, or construct something from a found object, such as a small fishing boat from a piece of driftwood. A contorted tree branch will take on the look of bleached and weathered timber if treated with a thin white colourwash, and fallen leaves and pine cones can be transformed by gilding.

Fruit and vegetables

Thread melon or sunflower seeds onto thick jute string and use them as curtain tie-backs. Allow gourds, squashes and pumpkins to dry out in a darkened space, then varnish them with shellac. Their natural ochre and sand tones will sing out from a plain white china bowl.

Baskets

An enormous range of woven baskets is now available in home-decorating stores and garden centres. Highly decorative as well as useful, they make ideal display containers for vibrantly coloured or richly textured fruits such as lemons and limes, kumquats and kiwis. An arrangement of pine cones, autumn leaves and seashells can look spectacular in a basket that complements the colours of the contents, and a stack of oversized stones in a generous log basket will make an impressive addition to the fireplace.

Glass

Turn glass tanks and vases into display cases overflowing with seashore finds, natural fabrics in a range of textures, buttons, tassels or silk ribbons. Or make a striking statement with a range of recycled glasses in vivid blues and greens across a window ledge or shelf, or atop a run of tongue-and-groove boarding.

Fabric bags and sachets

You can store or preserve dried leaves such as lavender and southernwood or bark chips in calico sachets hung from gingham or ticking ties.

SOURCES

GENERAL

After Noah
121 Upper St
London N1 1QP
Tel: 0171-379 6254
Original Arts and
Crafts furniture

The Conran Shop
Michelin House
81 Fulham Road
London SW3 6RD
Tel: 0171-589 7401
Wooden furniture,
unbleached cotton
fabric, lighting,
storage baskets

Eaton Shell Shop
30 Neal Street
Covent Garden
London
WC2H 9UE
Tel: 0171-379 6254
Shop and mail
order. Seashells,
woven cane blinds
and matting, raffia
bundles

Global Village
4th Floor
Harvey Nichols
109–125
Knightsbridge
London SW1
Tel: 0171-235 5000
Painted wood
furniture and fabric

Habitat
196 Tottenham
Court Road
London W1P 9LD
Tel: 0171-255 2545
Paper lampshades,
hand-dyed Indian
cottons, cane and
rattan furniture

Ikea
2 Drury Lane
Brent Park
North Circular
Road London
NW10 OTH
Tel: 0181-451 5566
Organic wood stains,
wallpapers, paper
lampshades,
recycled paper,
unbleached cotton
bedlinen and throws

The Kasbah
8 Southampton
Street
Covent Garden
London WC2
Tel: 0171-379 5230
Terracotta pots and
tiles, handwoven
rugs, cushions,
ornaments, paints

Cath Kidston
8 Clarendon Cross
London W11 4AP
Tel: 0171-221 4000
Original 50s
curtains, furniture
and bric-a-brac

John Lewis
Oxford Street
London W1A 1EX
Tel: 0171-629 7711

Liberty
Regent St
London W1R 6AH
Tel: 0171-734 123

Muji
26 Great
Marlborough Street
London W1V 1HI
Tel: 0171-494 1197
Simple Japanese
household items,
clothing and storage

Natural Fact
192 King's Road
London SW3 5XP
Tel: 0171-352 2227
Natural-inspired
furnishings

Old Town
32 Elm Hill
Norwich
Norfolk NR3 1HG
Tel: 01603 628100
Recycled kitchenalia
and workwear

Paperchase
Tel: 0171-580 8496
for nearest branch.
Recycled papers,
boxes and paper
products

Shaker
25 Harcourt St
London W1H 1DT
Tel: 0171-724 7672
Reproduction
Shaker furniture,
tin-ware and
accessories

Tobias & The Angel
6–8 White Hart Lane
London SW13 OPZ
Antique fabrics and
handmade
accessories

Traidcraft plc
Kingsway
Gateshead
Tyne and Wear
NE11 ONE
Tel: 0191 4910591
Ethical trader
supplying household
items and crafts
from developing
countries

Wong Singh Jones
253 Portobello Road
London W11
Tel: 0171-792 2001
Recycled tin
products

FLOORING

Crucial Trading
77 Westbourne
Park Road
London W2 4BX
Tel: 0171-221 9000
Natural matting

Elon
66 Fulham Road
South Kensington
London SW3 6HH
Tel: 0171-584 8966
Terracotta, slate,
glazed floor and
wall tiles

**European
Heritage Ltd**
56 Dawes Road
London SW6 7EJ
Tel: 0171-381 6063
Natural stone,
terracotta, ceramic,
marble and
handpainted tiles

Fired Earth
Twyford Mill
Oxford Road
Adderbury
Oxon OX17 3HP
Tel: 01295 812088
Tiles

**The Hardwood
Flooring Co Ltd**
146/152 West End
Lane, W. Hampstead
London NW6
New and reclaimed
parquet-block and
strip flooring

**Charles Hurst
Workshop**
Unit 21
Bow Triangle
Business Centre
Eleanor St
London N3 4NP
Tel: 0181-981 8562
High-quality tongue
-and-groove boarding

Natural Carpets
Oak House
Baughurst
Basingstoke
Hants RG26 5LP
Tel: 01345 585323
Seagrass, coir, sisal
and wool flatweave
flooring

Stonell Limited
Unit 1, Bockingfold
Ladham Road
Goudhurst
Kent TN17 1LY
Tel: 01580 211167
Limestone, slate,
marble, sandstone,
granite

**Three Shires
Natural Flooring**
3 Ptarmigan Place
Attleborough
Nuneaton
Warwickshire
CB11 6RX
Tel: 01203 370365
Sisal, seagrass, coir,
wool

**The Tintawn
Weaving Co**
Claire House
Bridge St
Leatherhead
Surrey
KT22 9BZ
Tel: 01372 363393
Natural wood
carpeting, natural
fibre coverings

Wicanders GB Ltd
Stoner House
Kilnmead
Crawley
W. Sussex
RH10 2BG
Tel: 01403 710001
Cork tiles

PAINTS

Annie Sloan Relics
35 Bridge St
Whitney OX8 6DA
Tel: 01993 704611
Traditional paints
and decorative
paint courses

Auro Organic Paints
Unit 1,Goldstones
Farm, Ashdon,
Saffron Walden
Essex CB10 2LZ
Tel: 01799 584888

**Brodie and
Middleton Ltd**
68 Drury Lane
London WC2B 5SP
Tel: 0171-836 3289
Theatrical paint
suppliers, powder
colours

L. Cornelissen & Son
105 Great Russell St.
London WC1B 3RY
Tel: 0171-636 1045
Paints, natural
pigments, artists'
materials

Craig & Rose plc
172 Leith Walk
Edinburgh EH6 5ER
Tel: 0131 554 1131
Paints

Farrow & Ball Ltd.
Voldens Trading
Estate, Wimborne
Dorset BH21 7NL
The National Trust
paint range

John Myland Ltd
80 Norwood
High Street
London SW27 9NW
Tel: 0181-670 9161
Paints and stains

**Nutshell Natural
Paints**
10 High Street
Totnes
Devon
Tel: 01803 867770
Natural distemper,
limewash and flat
oil paints, pigment
colours

Paint Magic
116 Sheen Road
Richmond
Surrey TW9 1UR
Tel: 0181-940 5503
Liming paste,
crackleglaze,
colourwash,
woodwash, verdigris

Papers & Paints
4 Park Walk
London SW10 0AD
Tel: 0171-352 8626
Organic paints,
stains and varnishes,
artists' materials

**E. Ploton
(Sundries) Ltd**
274 Archway Road
London N6 5AA
Tel: 0181-348 2838
Artists' materials
(mail order)

FITTINGS AND FURNISHINGS

Alphabeds
16 Broadway Market
London E8
Pine beds,
unbleached
mattresses

Damask
3–4 Broxholme
House
New Kings Road
Nr Harwood Road
London SW6
Tel: 0171-731 3553
Pure cotton
bedlinen,
patchwork quilts

Firifiss
PO Box 1464
Bournemouth
BH4 9YQ
Tel: 01202 753251
Cotton prints

**The Futon
Company**
138 Notting Hill
Gate
London W11
Tel: 0171-727 9252
Beds and bedding

**The Green
Catalogue**
Tel: 01931 732469
(Mail order)
Unbleached cotton
bedding; duvets
made from recycled
material

Ian Mankin
109 Regents Park
Road, Primrose Hill
London NW1
Tel: 0171-722 0997
Natural gingham,
ticking and other
cotton fabrics

**The Natural
Fabric Co**
Wessex Place
127 High St
Hungerford
Berkshire RG17 0DL
Tel: 01488 684002
Calico, ticking,
cotton, voile,
plain chintz
and silks

Old Town
32 Elm Hill,
Norwich
Tel: 01603 628100
Cotton gingham,
bedlinen, chambray
and tartan fabrics

Peter Reed Textiles
Springfield Mill
Churchill Way
Lomeshaye, Nelson
Lancashire BB9 6BT
100% cotton
bedlinen

V V Rouleaux
10 Symons St
London SW3
Tel: 0171-730 4413
Natural trimmings

The White Company
298-300 Munster Rd
London SW6 6BH
Bedlinens

Wotan Lamps Ltd
1 Gresham Way
Durnsford Road
London SW19 8HU
Lighting

Zeyko Kitchens
Half Moon
Courtyard
14 Chequer Street
St Albans, Herts
AL1 3YB
Environmentally
friendly kitchens

RECYCLED BUILDING MATERIALS
*For a list of salvage
dealers in Great
Britain contact:*

Salvo
Tel: 01225 445387

**London
Architectural Salvage
& Supply Company**
Mark St, Off Paul St
London EC2
Tel: 0171-739 0448

Walcot Reclamation
108 Walcot St
Bath BA1 5BG
Tel: 01225 444404

ENVIRONMENTAL ORGANIZATIONS

**Association of
Environment
Conscious Builders**
Windlake House
The Pump Field
Coaley, Glos.
GL11 5DX
Tel: 01453 890757

**The London
Ecology Centre**
45 Shelton St
London WC2H 9HJ
Tel: 0171-379 4324

Friends of the Earth
26–28 Underwood St
London N1 7JQ
Tel: 0171-490 155

CANADA

Up Country
247 Kind St. E
Toronto, Ontario
M5A 1J9

B.B. Bargoons
201 Whitehall Dr.
Markham, Ontario
L3R 9Y3

Ikea
15 Provost Dr.
North York, Ontario
M2K 2X9

NEW ZEALAND

Levene & Co. Ltd
Harris Road
East Tamaki
Auckland

The Store
114 Broadway
Newmarket
Auckland

INDEX

ACKNOWLEDGMENTS

The publisher thanks the following photographers and organizations for their kind permission to reproduce the photographs in this book:

2 Jean-Pierre Godeaut; **4–5** B. Touillon/ Côté Sud/Elizabeth Whiting & Associates; **5** centre right Marc Loiseau/Archipress; **5** below right Tim Goffe/Conran Octopus; **6** Henry Bourne/ Homes & Gardens/Robert Harding Syndication; **7** Eric Morin/ Côté Sud/ Elizabeth Whiting & Associates; **8** Jerome Darblay; **9** Gilles de Chabaneix/ Stylist: A.M. Comte & J. Postic/ Marie Claire Maison; **10** Ingalill Snitt; **11** Marie-Pierre Morel/Stylist: J. Postic/Marie Claire Maison; **12** Nicolas Tosi/Stylist: J. Borgeaud/ Marie Claire Maison; **13** Jerome Darblay; **14** Antoine Rozes; **15** Deidi von Schaewen; **17** Fritz von der Schulenburg/The Interior Archive; **18–19** Christoph Kicherer/Yves Marbrier (Apartment: Michele Oka Doner, New York); **20** Dominique Vorillon; **21** Jan Baldwin (Andrew Mortada); **22** Peter Cook/ Archipress (Architects: AD Partnership); **23** Jean-Pierre Godeaut; **24–25** James Merrell/ Woman's Journal/Robert Harding Syndication; **24** Ingalill Snitt; **26** Christian Sarramon; **27** Christian Sarramon; **28–9** Ingalill Snitt; **29** above Torsten Hogh/Homes & Gardens/Robert Harding Syndication/Artist Anne Vilsbøll; **29** below Torsten Hogh/Homes & Gardens/ Robert Harding Syndication/Artist Anne Vilsbøll; **30** Jean-Pierre Godeaut ; **31** Bernard Touillon/Côté Sud/Elizabeth Whiting & Associates; **32–33** Alexandre Bailhache/ Stylist: D. Rozensztroch/ Marie Claire Maison; **33** right Deidi von Schaewen; **34–5** Fritz von der Schulenburg/The Interior Archive (Designer: Mimmi O'Connell); **38** Torsten Hogh/Homes & Gardens/Robert Harding Syndication; **42–43** Studio Brackrock; **44** below John Miller; **44** above Antoine Rozes; **45** Fritz von der Schulenburg/The Interior Archive (Designer: Mimmi O'Connell); **46** Tom Leighton/Stylist: Sue Golden/Elle Decoration; **47** Fritz von der Schulenburg/ The Interior Archive (Designer: Richard Mudditt); **48** Simon Brown; **49** Jerome Darblay; **50** Fritz von der Schulenburg/The Interior Archive (Designer: Diane Lamberton); **51** Antoine Rozes; **52–3** above Simon McBride; **53** above right Yves Duronsoy/Côté Sud/Elizabeth Whiting & Associates; **53** below right Jean-Pierre Godeaut; **53** below left Fritz von der Schulenburg/The

Interior Archive (Designer: Mimmi O' Connell); **54** Fritz von der Schulenburg/The Interior Archive; **58–9** Studio Brackrock; **60** Ingalill Snitt; **61** Ingallil Snitt/Stylist: D. Rozensztroch/Marie Claire Maison; **62–3** Gilles de Chabaneix/Stylist: C. de Chabaneix & V. Meris/Marie Claire Idees; **63** right Christophe Dugied/Stylist: J. Postic/ Marie Claire Maison; **64** above left Bernard Touillon/Côté Sud/Elizabeth Whiting & Associates; **64** below left Bernard Touillon/Côté Sud/Elizabeth Whiting & Associates; **64–65** Jan Baldwin/Home & Gardens/Robert Harding Syndication; **66** below Simon Brown/The Interior Archive; **66** above Fritz von der Schulenburg/The Interior Archive (Designer: Mimmi O'Connell); **67** Christopher Drake/ Homes & Gardens/Robert Harding Syndication; **68–9** Ingalill Snitt; **69** right Debi Treloar/Homes & Gardens/Robert Harding Syndication; **70** Ingalill Snitt; **71** T. Jeanson/SIP/Elizabeth Whiting & Associates; **72** Christophe Dugied/ Stylist: P. Ricard-André/Marie Claire Maison; **73** Simon Wheeler/Elle Decoration; **74** above SIP/ Elizabeth Whiting & Associates; **74** below Cookie Kinkead; **75** Trevor Richards/Homes & Gardens/Robert Harding Syndication; **76–7** right Simon Wheeler/Elle Decoration; **76** left Antoine Rozes; **78** Christophe Dugied/Stylist: J.Postic/Marie Claire Maison; **79** Christophe Dugied/Stylist: J. Postic/Marie Claire Maison; **80** Habitat U.K. Limited; **81** Habitat U.K. Limited; **86–7** Jan Baldwin/ Homes & Gardens/ Robert Harding Syndication; **88–89** Alexandre Bailhache/ Stylist: D. Rozensztroch/Marie Claire Maison; **88** left Ingalill Snitt; **90** Jerome Darblay; **91** Fritz von der Schulenburg/The Interior Archive; **92** Marie-Pierre Morel/Stylist: C. Peuch/Marie Claire Maison; **93** Gilles de Chabaneix/ Stylist: D. Rozensztroch/Marie Claire Maison; **94–5** Alexandre Bailhache/ Stylist: J. P. Billaud/Marie Claire Maison; **95** right Ingalill Snitt; **96** Simon Kenny/Belle Magazine; **97** Simon Wheeler/Elle Decoration; **98–9** Simon Brown; **98** left Fritz von der Schulenburg/ The Interior Archive (Designer: Mimmi O'Connell); **100** Christophe Dugied/ Stylist: J. Postic/ Marie Claire Maison; **102–3** Paul Ryan/ Homes & Gardens/Robert Harding Syndication; **102** left Ingalill Snitt; **103** right W. Waldron/ SIP/Elizabeth Whiting & Associates; **104** Jan Baldwin (Andrew Mortada); **105** Tom

Leighton/Stylist: Sue Golden/Elle Decoration; **106–7** Richard Bryant/Arcaid (Madame Pommereau, Domaine de Sperone); **116** Pia Tryde/Homes & Gardens/Robert Harding Syndication; **117** James Merrell/Homes & Gardens/ Robert Harding Syndication; **118** Tom Leighton/Stylist: Sue Golden/Elle Decoration; **119** below Simon Brown/The Interior Archive; **120** left Jean Pierre Godeaut (J. Prisca); **120–1** Dominque Vorillon; **121** above Jean-Pierre Godeaut (Yuri Kuper); **121** below Simon Brown/The Interior Archive; **122** Christopher Drake/ Homes & Gardens/Robert Harding Syndication; **123** Marie-Pierre Morel/Stylist: G. Le Signe & C. Peuch/Marie Claire Maison; **124** Fritz von der Schulenburg/The Interior Archive (Designer: Mimmi O' Connell); **125** Jan Baldwin (Andrew Mortada); **126** Simon Brown/The Interior Archive; **127** below Hannah Lewis/ Stylist: Sue Parker/Elle Decoration; **127** above Hannah Lewis/Stylist: Sue Parker/Elle Decoration; **128** Above G. de Laubier/ SIP/ Elizabeth Whiting & Associates; **136** right Fritz von der Schulenburg/The Interior Archive; **136** left Gilles de Chabaneix/Stylist: D. Rozensztroch/Marie Claire Maison; **137** Right B. Touillon/Cote Sud/Elizabeth Whiting & Associates; **138** Jan Baldwin/ Homes & Gardens/Robert Harding Syndication ; **139** Simon Brown/The Interior Archive

The photographs on the following pages were taken specially for Conran Octopus by James Merrell, projects produced by Susan Skeen: 1, 5(top), 19, 36–7, 40–1, 43, 55–7, 59, 68, 82–5, 87, 101, 108, 110–12, 114–15, 119 (left), 128 (below), 129–35, 137 (left)

The authors would like to thank the following for their help: Carole Whittaker for checking the Fittings and Furnishings projects, Keith Harrison for checking the Walls, Floors, Windows & Doors and Display projects.

Props used in the front jacket photograph were provided by:
Designers Guild, 271 Kings Road, London SW3 5EN; Aero, 96 Westbourne Grove, London W2 5RT; Cath Kidston, 8 Clarendon Cross, London W11; Summerhill & Bishop, 100 Portland Road, London W11 4LN; Wild at Heart, 222 Westbourne Grove, London W11 2RJ